To Don Anderson —
Who has helped us to
see & know Him better —

Bill Austin
2001

The back of God

Signs of his presence

BILL AUSTIN

Tyndale House
Publishers, Inc.
Wheaton, Illinois

All Scripture quotations
are from the
King James Version
unless otherwise indicated.

Library of Congress
Catalog Card Number
79-67160.
ISBN 0-8423-0115-1,
paper.
Copyright © 1980
by Bill Austin.
All rights reserved.
First printing,
April 1980.
Printed in the
United States of America.

To the dedicated teachers
who demonstrated to me
that it is possible
for mind and heart
to coexist in faith

CONTENTS

PROLOGUE:
THROUGH A GLASS DARKLY

I want to see God. I need to see God. I am trying to see God. I am seeing God. I shall see God.

In various depths and endless varieties of spiritual searching, my soul seeks the face of God. In the darkness of despair I cry for one light to assure me that his face hovers near. In the brightness of joy I eagerly reach for his hand to join me in the dance of my happiness. In the uncertainty of decisions I plead for the wisdom of the ages which shines from his eyes. In the loneliness of my pilgrimage I listen for the soft voice of his companionship.

I am incomplete without him, yet I never know him completely. I am created to have fellowship with him, yet he often seems so far away. I am supposed to know and do his will, yet I seldom have the wisdom to know or the power to do. I am called repeatedly into his presence, yet when I arrive he seems to have moved on elsewhere. I am growing and developing a mature faith, yet I often feel childish, immature, and helpless. I am trying to learn from others who have traveled this way before me, yet I find that they have sometimes taken detours or evaded main thoroughfares. I am seeing God everywhere, yet I cannot hold the focus in any one place long enough to capture his image.

In my child-adult faith I am increasingly aware of the half-tones of revelation. I hear a voice but cannot tell its pitch or volume, and often its message is unclear. I see a distant figure I know I must follow after, but I cannot keep pace and the image fades in and out as though I were peering through a dense fog. I feel the wind of the Spirit and can hear the sound thereof, but I cannot tell whence it cometh or whither it goeth.

It seems that the more I know, the more I realize I do not know. Very personal and very pertinent have become these timeless words of the Apostle Paul: "For we know in part, and we prophesy in part. But when that which is perfect is come, then that which is in part shall be done away. *For now we see through a glass darkly*; but then face to face: now I know in part; but then shall I know even as also I am known" (1 Corinthians 13:9, 10, 12).

Should I then abandon all efforts to know more about God in this life? Am I wasting energy and time in the pursuit of that illusive Figure in the fog? Am I riding a merry-go-round of unanswered questions and insoluble problems? Should I learn to live with what I know and leave the rest to God and eternity?

I am strongly tempted to say that since I cannot know everything there is no need to try to learn anything more. It would be very comfortable to settle down with familiar thought patterns and accepted terminology. It would feel exceedingly secure to build a stockade fence around my present theology and hoard the treasure that I have thus far discovered. But I am "compassed about with so great a cloud of witnesses" that I must "run with patience the race that is set before me."

There are the witnesses of the restless men of faith before me who carved out from the wilderness of superstition and unbelief the theology which I have inherited. Their dedicated legacy demands that I continue the quest.

There are the witnesses of hungry laymen who look to their shepherds for feeding. So many have existed so long on the milk of the Word and are now crying out for the meat. Their hunger and their search demands that some of us try to offer a little more substance in their faith diet.

There are the witnesses of naive youth who feel that all knots should disappear when the string is pulled and that all problems should be solved once they have prayed. Their simplistic faith demands that one more word be added to their spiritual and intellectual preparation.

There are the biblical witnesses to the faith, who sought and found a higher peak of revelation on which to stand. Their successful odyssey into truth compels me to join their caravan and strike out on the quest for God. Standing out among all these biblical

heroes is Moses, the towering preeminent figure of
the Old Testament, the deliverer of Israel and giver
of the Law. Tucked away in the folds of a forgotten
incident on Sinai may be the very compass we need
to continue our venture into God.

*Moses said to the Lord, "Thou bidst me lead this people
up, but thou hast not told me whom thou wilt send with
me. Thou hast said to me, 'I know you by name, and further, you have found favour with me.' If I have indeed won
thy favour, then teach me to know thy way, so that I can
know thee and continue in favour with thee, for this nation
is thy own people." The Lord answered, "I will go with you
in person and set your mind at rest." Moses said to him,
"Indeed if thou dost not go in person, do not send us up from
here; for how can it ever be known that I and thy people
have found favour with thee, except by thy going with us?
So shall we be distinct, I and thy people, from all the peoples
on earth." The Lord said to Moses, "I will do this thing that
you have asked, because you have found favour with me,
and I know you by name."*

*And Moses prayed, "Show me thy glory." The Lord an-
swered, "I will make all my goodness pass before you, and I
will pronounce in your hearing the Name JEHOVAH. I
will be gracious to whom I will be gracious, and I will have
compassion on whom I will have compassion." But he added,
"My face you cannot see, for no mortal man may see me and
live." The Lord said, "Here is a place beside me. Take your
stand on the rock and when my glory passes by, I will put
you in a crevice of the rock and cover you with my hand
until I have passed by.* Then I will take away my hand,
and you shall see my back, but my face shall not be
seen" (Exodus 33:12-23, NEB).

Moses was not always on the mountaintop, seeing visions, hearing voices, receiving commandments. He knew the deep valleys of guilt and remorse. He had endured the howling wilderness of waste and purposelessness. He had spent countless days and nights with the desolation of the desert and the silence of the stars.

He thought he had seen his last personal valley when he reached Sinai, bringing the children of Israel to keep their appointment with their Deliverer God. Here they would bind themselves together with the One who had chosen them. Here the people of the promise would become the people of the covenant.

From this place they would move on to Canaan and possess the land which had been promised to Abraham and his descendants. It was a grand plan, and Moses' soul had stood on tiptoe in eagerness to see it all fulfilled.

But something had happened. The people were not yet a covenant people. The very words which constituted the core of the covenant were shattered into pieces when Moses flung the tables of stone to the bottom of Sinai. He had reacted in righteous fury to the spectacle of sensuality and idolatry before his eyes.

While Moses had been on the mount, receiving the Ten Commandments, the people had become impatient and had lost faith in the enterprise. They persuaded Aaron, Moses' brother and co-leader, to fashion a golden calf to worship in place of the living God who had brought them there. Then the people followed the idolatrous worship with the customary dancing, frivolity, and sexual orgies. It was this primitive, unrestrained debauchery that greeted Moses as he came down from Sinai with the sacred Law tucked under his arms.

Now he sat alone and disconsolate in his personal tent at the foot of Sinai. After severely punishing the people for their apostasy, Moses had moved his tent outside the camp toward the low rolling foothills of Sinai. He could not afford to leave the people again; they needed his strong hand and spiritual guidance more than ever. He designated his tent as the Tabernacle of the Congregation, or the "Tent of the Presence." Those who desired an audience with God were told to come to Moses' tent, except when they saw the pillar of cloud enfolding the tent, indicating God's presence and his private audience with Moses.

It was during one of these special divine visitations to Moses' tent that the venerable prophet and national leader poured out the frustrations of his soul. He could not forget the earlier sensation of communing with God on the mountain; but neither could he shake the depression brought on by the people's defection. The centuries-long dream seemed to have ended. His heart kept telling him to believe, but his mind was full of unanswered questions. Although he had been blessed as no other man with special revelation, he was still human, and he shared with all humanity the time of despair.

Moses stands tall in mankind's story of faith, *not* because he never knew despair, but because of what he did with his despair. He took it directly to God and bared every jagged edge of his anxiety.

He complained that God had not told him enough about the promised divine guidance. He insisted on some kind of assurance that he and the people of Israel had really been chosen by God. Finally, he cried out to God, "Show me thy glory." His cry voiced the groanings of his despair and the questions of his anxiety.

His cry is Everyman's cry. From the simple flowered paths of Eden to the concrete jungle of Metropolis, men have cried for God to show his glory, to reveal himself in some clear, tangible, unmistakable way. Even the greatest in faith still yearn to see more and know more of the God in whom they believe.

Our prayers may be for health or success, for faith or renewal, for guidance or comfort, but at the heart of them all, what we are asking is that God show himself strong and right and pure. We are convinced that everything will be all right in the drama of our lives if and when God comes on stage. Therefore, we hear ourselves joining the chorus of Moses, crying for God to show his glory.

Standing with Moses on the windswept slopes of Sinai, we hear the bold words bouncing from rock to crevice and tumbling over themselves in hollow echoes: "Show me thy glory . . . thy glory . . . glory. . . ." The following silence is heavy and ominous, until broken and replaced with a calm, patient, loving voice.

Deliberately, unhurriedly, the God of Abraham, Isaac, and Jacob speaks to Moses (and through him to us?). He tells Moses that he will cause the goodness of God to pass before him, will pronounce his name unto him and will exercise his sovereign grace. But he adds that Moses cannot see his face, "for no mortal man may see me and live."

God proceeds to tell Moses that he will place him in a crevice of a rock and cover the creature's eyes with the Creator's hand while he passes by. Then God says that he will remove his hand and Moses will be able to see his back, but not his face.

The back of God! Is this what the prophet and deliverer of Israel gets for his faithful service? Is this the total discovery of a lifetime search? Is this an adequate answer for all the ultimate questions?

If a man as close to God as Moses can get no more than a glimpse of his back, what hope is there for *us* to really encounter this God of the Bible? And yet, the limitations and frustrations of Moses remind us that he was an authentic human being and not just a celluloid hero. If he was real as we are real, then perhaps we can share some of the reality of his encounter with God. Perhaps he can help us learn how God reveals himself; and wouldn't it be wonderful if he could teach us how to read the signs God gives us? We might see a new purpose to our lives and a new vision of God's will even while acknowledging that "now we see through a glass darkly."

ONE
The Hidden Depths of Many a Heart

Oh, teach me, Lord, that I may teach
The precious things Thou dost impart;
And wing my words that they may reach
The hidden depths of many a heart.

from the hymn
Lord, Speak to Me
by Frances R. Havergal

*If I have indeed won thy favour, then teach me to know thy
way, so that I can know thee and continue in favour with
thee* (Exodus 33:13, NEB).

ONLY THOSE who have been patient through the
years understand the urgency of the hour.

Moses was eighty years old, and every step of
every day of every year had been a tedious, but necessary, part of the journey to this place and this time.
He had not always known where his steps were leading him, or whether he wanted to go there, but he
had felt drawn by a destiny that provided its own
force.

Patience was not among his original equipment.
Eager to be a deliverer before God had tutored him
for that delicate vocation, he had impulsively slain an
Egyptian overseer who was abusing an Israelite slave.

To escape the reprisal of Pharaoh, Moses fled to the deserts of Midian where he enrolled in a forty-year course in patience and silence.

On the sacred ground around the burning bush, Moses discarded his shoes and his solitude. Obeying the instructions of God, he left the back side of the desert for the forefront of the battle. In the coarse garb of a bedouin shepherd, he strode into Pharaoh's opulent palace, demanding that he let the Israelites go.

Holding the line for God's terms against the stubborn Pharaoh, Moses refused to bargain with even a fraction of his people's freedom. After the land had been decimated by plague upon plague, the Israelites marched out of the land of their bondage, with the stench of death hovering behind them. After four hundred years of insufferable existence as nonpersons, a nation was born in a day.

The exodus was climaxed by the miraculous crossing of the mighty sea, and celebrated with the high song of Moses and the happy dancing of Miriam. In the long trek across the wilderness, the new nation survived thirst, hunger, bitter waters, and bitter attitudes. They fought and won their first battle as a united people. They learned the fine art of organization from Moses' father-in-law, and they came at last to the holy mountain called Sinai.

It was here that Moses had encountered the God of the burning bush, and it was here that God had told him he would make a covenant with his people. The symbol of the covenant, the stone-etched law, had been shattered when Moses returned to find the people in rebellious debauchery.

In the long, quiet days that followed, Moses spent endless hours in the Tent of the Presence, searching his heart and seeking his God. As he retraced his steps back over the long pilgrimage of faith, he felt he had the right to ask more of God.

He knew he was a sinner, and never forgot it. But he also knew that he had been obedient to the heavenly vision. He had done all that God had told him before Pharaoh, Egypt, and Israel. He had believed when the people lost faith. He had prayed while the people murmured. He had forged ahead when the people wanted to turn back. He was in the very presence of God while the people were constructing an idol to worship.

Moses had learned how to be patient with God, with people, and with himself. He had waited years for his mission assignment and months for its emerging shape. He knew that too much was invested in this enterprise to let it perish by default.

The long years of patient faithfulness had convinced him of the importance of this present crisis. The people must recover, the covenant must be made, the promised land must be occupied.

The urgency of the hour was thus born, not out of impulsive restlessness, but out of a soul's commitment to accomplish his mission and bring ultimate issues to a divine fulfillment.

It was really quite simple, at last, for Moses. He knew he was standing *where* he should, *as* he should. If he had found favor with God, he wanted God to reveal his way to him now, and show him where to place his foot in the next step. He had come as far as he could; the next move was up to God.

WANTING TO KNOW HIS WAY

Knowing what to ask for helps us recognize the answer when it comes.

Moses felt a very specific need at this juncture and he placed that need before God in a specific request. He said, "Thou bidst me lead this people up, but thou hast not told me whom thou wilt send with me" (Exodus 33:12, NEB).

In verse 2, God had reminded Moses that he would "send an angel" before him on the way to Canaan, and in verse 12, Moses is asking God to identify precisely who this angel is to be.

The first mention of the promised angel occurs in Exodus 23:20, in the midst of various laws and ordinances. God said, "Behold, I send an Angel before thee, to keep thee in the way, and to bring thee into the place which I have prepared." Then he gave instructions for the Israelites to obey the angel, with

the warning that disobedience would make God himself their enemy.

The angel promise is repeated in Exodus 32:34,
after Moses had interceded for the people, asking
God to forgive their shameful apostasy at the base of
Sinai. The last reference, Exodus 33:2, is almost
identical, word for word, with the promise in Exodus
23:23. Names are given of the specific nations which
will be driven out before the angel.

Who is this mysterious angel which keeps coming
up in the conversations between God and Moses?
Well, that is precisely what Moses wants to know.
He is not simply curious; he is desperate to have definite knowledge and reassurance. In effect, he is saying to God in 33:12, "You have given me the assignment of taking the people to Canaan, and you keep
promising me that your angel will go with us. But
who is this angel? How will I recognize the divinely
appointed guide? Give me something more tangible
and concrete than this vague promise of an angel's
presence."

It is not the first time the great Moses reveals that
he has feet of clay, but in this particular encounter,
he wears boldly the badge of humanity. In this cry
for concrete evidence, we recognize the human frustration that is also ours. We hear a giant of faith
plead for proof and it sounds like the echo of our own
anguish. Why must we be satisfied with promises
when our needs demand fulfillment? Why are we
given symbols when our lives crave reality? Moses
has struck a universal chord and the resulting note is
the wail of "the hidden depths of many a heart."

The exposure of Moses' imperfect faith may be the illumination we need by which to see and understand more clearly the back of God. If we can truly accept the full humanity of this towering hero of the Bible, perhaps we can better accept the full message of his encounter.

It is our natural tendency to place the biblical characters in a special category, different from the people of secular history, and certainly different from us. If we can work through the mystery of revelation and the miracles of deity, back to the human beings who were involved, we will relate better both to them and to their God. We are so overwhelmed by the intervention of the supernatural in the biblical records that we often do not see the natural context in which it was taking place.

I may not understand this voice or that vision, or some miracle, but I must not let this mystery obscure the real and normal humanity of the persons affected. It is good for me to hear Moses doubting and demanding more proof. I know he did not have some special intuitive equipment or walk in some other-worldly atmosphere. I can see myself in that lonely figure silhouetted against the gray-brown sky of Sinai. I can hear my own prayer of a half-born faith crying, "Lord, I believe; help thou my unbelief!"

Believing and not believing. Trusting and doubting. Reaching for heaven and holding tightly to earth. Accepting God's Word and asking for proof. This is my bondage that will not let me soar above every doubt and resolve every question; but it is also my link with the forefathers of faith. They were every bit as human as I am, and sought as insistently for facts as I do.

The mistake I am prone to make is to *stop* with comparing my human limitations to theirs. If I can identify with their doubts, why can't I *move on* to experience their faith? If I can say that I certainly know how Moses felt, because I often feel that way, why can't I accept God's response to Moses as also applying to me? I rob myself of life's richest possibilities when I stop with the human situation and do not press on to the divine solution.

Moses says, "Lord, I'm sorry, but I need to know more," and I say, "Lord, I'm just like Moses; I need to know more, too." Now, am I willing to listen, and learn, and live according to what I hear next?

God's answer to Moses was simple but conclusive, "My presence shall go with thee, and I will give thee rest" (v. 14). This apparently settled the issue with Moses. He never again asked God about the angel, and God never mentioned the subject again.

Many attempts have been made to understand this promise and to identify the angel. The word angel means "messenger" and may or may not refer to a supernatural being. Contemporary with Moses was the idea that an angel was an intermediary, one who appeared as a nonhuman figure to lead God's people, such as the angel of God's leadership at the crossing of the sea (Exodus 14:19, ff.). Whatever form the angel assumed, it is obvious that Moses is expecting some similar manifestation. On the other hand, since

Moses asked to know "whom" God would send with them, he may have been looking for an identifiable human helper.

Some Jewish commentators consider Moses himself to have been the angel God sent to lead Israel, and that Moses was blind to that arrangement at first. Some Christian commentators spiritualize the designation to be that of one of the persons of the Trinity, suggesting even that it referred to the preexistent Christ. More practical-minded scholars have interpreted the Ark of the Covenant as the embodiment of the promise since it went before the tribes, bore the revelation of God, and symbolized the presence of God (Numbers 10:33, ff.).

The diligent search and educated speculations about the identity of the angel are likely to obscure the central point of the issue, which is that Moses was apparently satisfied with God's simple explanation, "*My* presence shall go with thee." It is as though a new understanding of God's omnipresence flooded over Moses. Is it possible that his primitive faith was just now grasping the concept of a God who is always with us, who does not have to be summoned from his quarters to attend our needs?

One of the early patriarchs of Israel—Jacob—had obviously not understood that about the God his grandfather Abraham worshiped. In the desert alone, he dreamed of a vast ladder stretching between heaven and earth, with angels ascending and descending. At the top he saw God, who repeated the Abrahamic covenant promise to him. Awakening, Jacob exclaimed reverently, "Surely the Lord is in this place; and I knew it not" (Genesis 28:16).

Perhaps the dialogue between God and Moses reflects the developing theology of Israel. We can be quite certain that the Ark of the Covenant was needed as a symbol of God's omnipresence because the people had discovered God at Sinai and were reluctant to leave. How could they be sure he would stay with them? Would they need to return annually to the sacred mountain for a renewed revelation?

These questions must have plagued the people until God gave them the assurance of the ark and the portable tabernacle. Through these he was saying, "I will go with you. I will never forsake you nor leave you." How far Moses had personally grown in his comprehension of God's omnipresence we do not know, but we do know that he never asked again about the angel.

Many of us have not yet grown beyond asking about the angel. It is not enough that God has promised to bless us; we want to know how and how much. It is not enough that he has promised to send the Comforter; we want to see signs of his presence. It is not enough that he has promised to be with us until the end of the world; we want him to change the world more to our liking. After these many centuries of testimony to his power and presence, we insist on seeing and hearing him now.

Contrary to natural laws, it is through believing that we see, not through seeing that we believe. Only he who takes God at his word can translate the word when he receives it. Frantic beating does not force the door open, but patient waiting is rewarded with perfectly timed access to new truths. Why should we insist that God give us more of himself when we have not accepted what he has already given? Rather than demanding more knowledge and increased power, let us realize the full potential of what we already have.

Centuries after Moses, the Christ would emphasize stewardship of the present status in his parable of the talents and the unfruitful fig tree. He would feed a multitude, not with the bounty of men's intentions, but with the available lunch of a small lad. He would not wait for an educated and trained cadre to begin his church; he would start with the ready rag-tag group at hand. He would not wait for men to appreciate or understand his sacrifice; he would die for them because nothing less could redeem them.

It is commendable, even essential, that the people of God want always to learn more of their God, to "grow in wisdom and in the nurture of the Lord Jesus," to "study to show themselves approved unto God." But it is more important that we act in faith on the knowledge we already have. God may be waiting to show us the next step to take because we have not yet taken the last one he showed us.

God did not tell Moses who the angel would be, but he promised his own personal presence, and Moses acted in faith on that promise and brought his people to Canaan land. Those who insist on having their angel may miss God himself. Which is better, to have only what we can see, or to have the unseen treasures and unknown power of God at our constant disposal? We may not be intellectually satisfied at not knowing the mystery of the angel, but Moses was more than satisfied when he heard God say, "Moses, don't worry about that angel. I myself am with you!" No man can be a Moses until he's ready to settle for that answer.

NEEDING TO
KNOW WE BELONG

The assurance of acceptance is the most fundamental element of emotional stability.

Even after all the miraculous interventions in behalf of Israel, Moses did not take their relationship with God for granted. When God answered his inquiry about the angel with the promise of his personal presence, Moses immediately exclaimed, "Indeed if thou dost not go in person, do not send us up from here; for how can it ever be known that I and thy people have found favour with thee, except by thy going with us? So shall we be distinct, I and thy people, from all the peoples on earth" (Exodus 33:15, 16, NEB).

When we heard Moses ask for more information about God's plan, we may have been prone to think he was merely concerned about their safety or the success of their mission. Now, however, we move in

on a deeper level of his concern. He wasn't asking for
protection; he was after the seal of acceptance.

Security may be enough for the animals of the forest as they defeat or evade their enemies, retreating
into protective seclusion. But the human animal,
made in the image of God, is never satisfied until he
has fellowship with other human beings, and even
with the Creator himself.

Success may be enough for the person who oper-
ates on the premise that the end justifies the means.
But the caring person, who knows himself to be part
of the greater community, is never satisfied until relationships reflect trust and acceptance.

A pragmatic world too readily condemns sensi-
tivity as vulnerability. We are told that we should be
self-sufficient, build fences to shelter our emotions,
and aspire to independence as the ultimate maturity.
Am I immature to confess that I need affirmation?
Am I too sensitive when I am hurt because of rejection or misunderstanding? Am I childish and vulnerable because I expose my emotions when I feel
deeply?

Isn't it just possible that I am the most mature
when I am admitting that there are significant others
in my world on whom I greatly depend? My confessed need for acceptance may be an intelligent
awareness that my world is bigger than my own
backyard. My prayer to God for a sign of his ap-
proval ought to be seen as evidence of a man growing
out of his self-centeredness into God-consciousness.

When Moses cried out to God for proof that he
and Israel were chosen by God, distinct from all

other people, he openly and unashamedly confessed their need for confirmation and affirmation. He was expressing another universal and basic need from "the hidden depths of many a heart," perhaps the greatest need of all—the need to belong.

The assurance of primary belonging, however, does not issue from identity with a compatible and respectable group. Moses was concerned first of all that he belonged to God, not just to a peer group with rich religious heritage. If we are content in our sense of acceptance because we are comfortably associated with a desirable church, or because we feel a special camaraderie with a small core group, we may be using the wrong standards.

If I look hard enough I can find someone somewhere who will agree with my ideas, regardless of how unorthodox they may be. Acceptance by other misguided souls does not turn heresy into truth. If I try earnestly I can find someone somewhere who is eager to start a new church, ready to denounce all churches, willing to accept everything without change, or determined to change everything. A group of people getting together with wrong ideas only multiplies error, never corrects it. Authentic acceptance, biblical acceptance, everlasting acceptance, comes from a right relationship with God, not just belonging to a crowd that thinks like I do.

Neither does the assurance of primary belonging come to us through family and ancestors. The bones of the great Joseph accompanied the people in their Exodus adventure (Exodus 13:19); but that did not make them holy. Joseph's father was Jacob, whose

name was changed to Israel, the name by which the
nation is known to this day, but that did not make
them holy. Jacob's father was Isaac, the child of
promise who had been miraculously spared to continue the seed, but that did not make them holy.
Isaac's father was Abraham, who had been the first
called and the father of many nations, but that did
not make them holy.

Holiness cannot be inherited. Even a promise from
God is not transferable. He had pronounced his first
covenant pledge to Abraham, promising Canaan to
his descendants (Genesis 12:7). But the pledge had to
be renewed and restated to Isaac, for he could not inherit his father's relationship to God (Genesis 26:24).
Then the pledge was repeated again to Jacob, Isaac's
son, as though for the first time (Genesis 28:13, 14).
It is the same God, keeping the same covenant, but
each man receives it for himself.

Moses knows that. He knows that the people cannot march up to Canaan, assuming that the land is
theirs just because Abraham was their forefather. He
prays, therefore, for a more conclusive assurance of
acceptance than the heritage of the past. Is this not a
foretaste of that Christian gospel which would one
day proclaim that true children of God cannot be
produced by human blood lines but only by the
Heavenly Father himself? (John 1:12, 13.)

Family genealogy cannot replace personal theology. Respect for history helps us to know where we
have come from, but only a present experience can
assure us of where we are going. While God is invit-
ing us to become members of his family, it doesn't

seem very wise for us to insist that our earthly families are quite adequate. Let us be grateful for the influence of our forefathers and present family, but pay them the greatest tribute of all by trusting in the God to whom they have pointed us, and not in our relationship to them.

Just as the assurance of primary belonging cannot be found in the positive relationships of godly heritage, neither can it be found in the negative knowledge of the misfortune of others. A deceptive thought process has begun when we think that we must be right or "chosen" because we do not suffer as others do. True faith has no place for such slogans as "might is right," "bigger is better," or "good guys always win."

The cross of Christ is the climactic testimony of a long history of injustices which seem to hint that the chosen ones may be chosen for suffering.

Moses knew the Israelites were already forgetting their four hundred years bondage in Egypt, and were gloating over the destruction of the Egyptians. Hadn't God shown favoritism in the plagues? When it was dark in Egypt, it was not dark where the Israelites lived. Egyptian cattle died, but not Israelite cattle. The first-born of every Egyptian family was stricken by the death angel, but the Israelite homes were spared.

Perhaps they had not remembered that the death angel passed over their homes because they had individually been obedient in preparing the Passover lamb and putting the blood on the doorposts. Even in the midst of national deliverance, personal faith was required.

Surely, by now, they had experienced enough
hunger and thirst and fear and loneliness and despair
and sin to know that chosen ones cannot be identified
by a life of ease and prosperity. Surely they were
more knowledgeable than to say, "We will always be
blessed by God; just look at what he did to the Egyptians."

My health is not guaranteed by my neighbor's dis-
ease, and my victory is not assured by my enemy's
defeat. God may be working on levels far beyond my
comparative analysis of success and failure. He may
be charting the course of others down paths totally
unrelated to my personal pilgrimage. To gauge the
level of my righteousness and divine acceptance by
the degree of someone else's welfare is the shakiest
foundation on which to build my assurance of belonging.

Neither is the sense of primary belonging to be
found in the sanctuary of private peace. To escape
"the madding crowd" and retreat to seclusion for personal devotion is tempting and usually refreshing. It
can, however, delude us into thinking this is the ultimate, that he who can find peace with himself has
found God. Some mystic religions may rely only on
meditation and introspection, but not the Christian
faith. Our God is Emmanuel, "God with us," plunging headlong into his sin-sick world, and thrashing
painfully on Calvary, "where cross the crowded ways
of life."

Moses knew that a chosen people could never be
smugly satisfied with their secret of chosenness. His
application for the credentials of chosenness was amplified by the plaintive plea, "How can it ever be

known that I and thy people have found favour with thee?" He made a strong point, as though to inform the Lord that the presence of the Almighty would stamp them as "distinct from all the peoples on earth." He fully understood that the faith of the people of God was intended to be a public testimony to the rest of the world.

A private, quiet, even secret religious faith may be aesthetically appealing, but it is not in the vein and spirit of biblical faith. Old Testament prophets called for men to openly choose which god they would serve (Joshua 24:14, 15; 1 Kings 18:21). Jesus Christ clearly stated that he would acknowledge in heaven those who acknowledged him on earth (Matthew 10:32, 33). Secret discipleship is not an option for the Christian. Following Christ begins with open confession. We are not chosen to keep our faith to ourselves, but to share it with a waiting, watching world.

Simply professing to believe, however, is not the certification for belonging. Jesus said, "Not everyone who calls me 'Lord, Lord' will enter the kingdom of Heaven, but only those who do the will of my heavenly Father" (Matthew 7:21, NEB). The true believer is identified eventually by what he does more than by what he says.

When Moses underscored the necessity for Israel to be "*distinct* from all the peoples of the earth," he was articulating the biblical principle of identity by distinction. The people of God are to be distinctly different from the people of the world. The New Testament makes no less a demand for such dedication. Paul quotes God as saying, "Come away and leave them, *separate* yourselves . . . touch nothing unclean. Then I will accept you . . . I will be a father to you, and you shall be my sons and daughters" (2 Corinthians 6:17, 18, NEB).

Paul finds the offer of God's loving relationship so magnificent that he cannot imagine we would shrink from the idea of being different for Christ's sake. He exclaims, "Such are the promises that have been made to us, dear friends. Let us therefore cleanse ourselves from all that can defile flesh or spirit, and in the fear of God complete our consecration" (2 Corinthians 7:1, NEB).

Are we to infer, then, that our assurance of belonging comes from a state of moral righteousness? Is our salvation attained by works, rather than grace? Not at all, for the distinctive set-apartness for which Moses (and Paul) contend is the result and evidence of the presence and grace of God!

This was the very heart and substance of Moses' plea: "If we do not have God's presence, how will the world know we have found his favor [grace]? If he does not go with us, how can we be distinct [consecrated] from the rest of the world?" It is a complete trusting in the grace of God alone. It is a total confession of human inadequacy. It is a death blow to any hope of salvation by humanism or socialism. The basic, indispensable ingredient for belonging is a trusting relationship with the God of grace, which results in an awareness of his presence.

God understands our need to know we belong. He understands the heart-wrenching cry of Moses. He did not condemn him for insisting on knowing God was with them. On the contrary, he replied, "I will do this thing that you have asked, because you have found favour with me, and I know you by name" (Exodus 33:17, NEB).

It was a gracious response, indeed, but still not enough for Moses. He had settled the issue of having to know about the angel, and he had cleared up the question of belonging, but an insatiable craving for absolute proof rumbled in his soul. He had one more question he knew he had to ask.

ASKING TO SEE HIS GLORY

Little men ask for trivial trinkets, but great men of faith hold out for the ultimate gift, God himself.

Moses had no awe for the prestige of human power; he snapped his finger in the face of Pharaoh. He attached no value of wealth to the gold men craved; he squandered it in the liquid-penalty he had made the Israelites drink. He did not need signs and wonders to convince him of God's power; his journey from Sinai's burning bush back to Sinai's Ten Commandments had been landmarked by miracle after miracle.

The heart-prayer of Moses was not for position or wealth or miracles. The deepest cry of his soul was to know God in all his fullness, to experience his unmistakable presence, to see his glory!

In Hebrew the word glory is *kabod* and in Greek it is *doxa*. From the Greek word we get our musical designation of "Doxology." When we sing our doxologies we are praying for, and paying homage to, the divine presence or glory of God.

In both the Hebrew and Greek, the word we translate "glory" means "presence, weight, or substance." It means more than the fact that one can answer the roll call that he is present. It means that his presence is obvious and materially experienced by all. In the tribal councils of Israel, a venerable father of faith would stride in with great *kabod*, and the people would know that a respected presence and a heard voice was among them. In the Greek empires a prominent landowner or a famous warrior would stand to speak in the assemblies, and all would feel his *doxa*, his weight, his substance, his presence.

The glory of God means more than a glittering majesty, it means the very essence of God himself. In Old Testament times, the glory of God would have been understood as a synonym for the face of God. Moses apparently desired to apprehend the full nature of God, to experience his burning presence, to see his glory, even his face. To see the face is to see the whole of the person, and this was obviously the intention of Moses' prayer. He wanted God to disclose himself completely.

Is a man ever satisfied with God's disclosure? Will he always be asking for more evidence, another sign, additional clues? Is there a certain kind of revelation that is conclusive? Is there a point in the communication between man and God at which man is willing to ask no more? Should there be?

My mind juggles these questions back and forth as

my heart tries to find a steady rock on which to
stand. I believe completely and yet my faith is not
complete. I believe God is everywhere but I have not
found him everywhere. I believe he is in all things,
but I know too many things that seem so godless.

I remember that God was adequate for yesterday's
problems and I trust him with tomorrow's worries,
but why can't I see him at work today?

I have a sense of his presence, but how do I know
this is not a subjective feeling instead of an objective
reality? When I say that I "know" God, I mean it in
a spiritual, rather than a physical sense. There has
been no empirical manifestation so that I could experience his presence as I do that of another human
being. I cannot produce photographic records of his
visits to me. Does this weaken the credibility of my
testimony? Does it weaken even my own faith in my
"experience" of God?

From this level of personal inquiry must eventually
come the question of how much revelation is necessary: necessary to convince me that there really is a
God and that he has really visited me; necessary for
others to be convinced that I have had an authentic
encounter with God and not just a psychological development. How much and what kind of God's glory
would do this?

Moses furnishes the best answer, because he came
the closest that man has ever come to full disclosure.
"And there arose not a prophet since in Israel like
unto Moses, whom the Lord knew face to face, in all
the signs and the wonders, which the Lord sent him
to do in the land of Egypt to Pharaoh, and to all his

servants, and to all his land, and in all that mighty hand, and in all the great terror which Moses showed in the sight of all Israel" (Deuteronomy 34:10–12).

But, unbelievable as it sounds, that was still not enough for Moses. He had seen the burning bush, heard the voice of the Lord, and gone to Egypt believing. He had seen ten devastating plagues thoroughly inundate the land of Egypt. He had seen water turn to blood, darkness cover the earth, and death strike where the blood was not. He had seen a pillar of fire terrorize the Egyptian army, and the Red Sea drown them. He had watched the waters roll back as a huge wall and his people walk through on dry land. He had seen bitter water made sweet and dry rock gush with a fountain. He had gathered manna from heaven and great coveys of quail for the people to eat. He had seen the Amalekites destroyed in battle as he kept his arms lifted unto Jehovah. He had seen the finger of God carve the commandments in tables of stone, and he had communed with him every day in the Tent of the Presence.

Yet he wanted to see more! Moses, how much does it take? How do you have the audacity to ask God for more? Why do you need to see the fullness of his glory? Haven't you seen enough? Oh, that any one of us could have just one portion of one of your miraculous days; it would satisfy us for all time and eternity!

Ah, but would it satisfy us? How can we possibly say that we would have more faith than Moses, be more surely convinced than he, be more blessedly content with whatever revelations? The point is that we cannot. Man can never be fully satisfied as long as he is on earth and God is in heaven—that is, until we see him in the full manifestation that awaits us there.

Physical evidence is not the solution to man's spiritual problem. Even the physical incarnation of God in Christ is not enough for men; it was not enough even for his disciples while he was with them in the flesh. "Philip said to him, 'Lord, show us the Father and we ask no more.' Jesus answered, 'Have I been all this time with you, Philip, and you still do not know me? Anyone who has seen me has seen the Father'" (John 14:8, 9, NEB).

Neither will miracles and spectacular wonders convince men that God is and that he loves them. The rich man pleaded for Abraham to send Lazarus back to earth to warn his brothers of hell. "But Abraham said, 'They have Moses and the prophets; let them listen to them.' 'No, father Abraham,' he replied, 'but if someone from the dead visits them, they will repent.' Abraham answered, 'If they do not listen to Moses and the prophets they will pay no heed even if someone should rise from the dead'" (Luke 16:29-31, NEB).

Is it wrong, then, for man to seek God? Is it useless for us to yearn for a closer look at the Almighty? Again, Moses would be our best source for an answer, and his emphatic answer would be, "No, it is not wrong, it is not useless to seek God!" Even though he kept wanting more, and although God would not give full disclosure, Moses still knew enough about God to know it was worth a lifetime of seeking to spend one minute in his presence.

Forty years after his mountain encounter with God, the old shepherd-prophet stood before a new generation of Israelites to prepare them for their entrance into Canaan. He rehearsed all the events of the great exodus so they would never forget, and he warned them of hazardous days ahead. Then he drew deep from the wells of his own personal experience to encourage them: "But if from thence thou shalt seek the Lord thy God, thou shalt find him, if thou seek him with all thy heart and with all thy soul" (Deuteronomy 4:29).

Centuries later, settled in the conquered land, their descendants would hear their shepherd-king David repeat the same admonition: "Seek the Lord, and his strength: seek his face evermore" (Psalm 105:4).

Then would come the clarion call of the prophet Isaiah, "Seek ye the Lord while he may be found, call ye upon him while he is near" (Isaiah 55:6). The compassionate Hosea would add his plea, "It is time to seek the Lord, till he come and rain righteousness upon you" (Hosea 10:12).

Even after the Messianic prophecies were fulfilled, the Christ himself would speak of the continuing necessity to seek, "For every one that asketh receiveth; and he that seeketh findeth; and to him that knocketh it shall be opened" (Luke 11:10). When the Apostle Paul would come to Athens to address the learned, he would echo the message to all men, "That they should seek the Lord, if haply they might feel after him, and find him, though he be not far from every one of us" (Acts 17:27).

Far from discouraging or condemning those who
seek God, the Scriptures consistently urge that men
make this the major pursuit of life. God did not reject Moses' seeking heart; he rewarded it. Although
he could not fully disclose all of himself in one place
to one man, he gave him all the revelation, inspira-
tion, and knowledge he needed for the task to which
he had called him.

The secret of spiritual satisfaction is willingness to
accept the given.

When God gives, man must be willing to accept
the gift. He cannot demand another gift which he
may prefer. Neither can he set about to obtain it for
himself. That which comes from God is given; it is
neither earned nor achieved. Our problem begins
when we say, "That's not what I wanted, Lord," or
"I think I'll keep working at it until I come up with
something better."

Moses took his burden to the Lord and left it
there. He never again asked to see God's glory. He
was obviously satisfied with the given of God. Of
course, he asked many times what God wanted him
to do in certain matters, but never again did he ask
for full manifestation of the divine presence. He realized that God knew how much he needed and could
manage, and he was therefore satisfied with what he
got.

In that sense he got what he asked for. A real
prayer is not so much to gain an object as it is to fill a
need. If I pray for medicine it is because my body is
sick. If my body is well when the medicine arrives, I

have no need for the medication for which I prayed; and yet, my real prayer—for restored health—has been abundantly answered.

If I pray that God perform a certain deed in order that I might believe, the real prayer is for faith, which very likely might come without the requested deed. So now I can be satisfied with my new faith in him.

Perhaps this is what happened to Moses. He didn't get exactly what he asked for, but he got all that he needed. The emptiness that had prompted the prayer in the first place was now filled with enough of God to last a lifetime.

TWO

He Will Make It Plain

Blind unbelief is sure to err,
And scan his work in vain:
God is his own interpreter
And he will make it plain.

from the hymn
God Moves in a Mysterious Way
by William Cowper

I will do this thing that you have asked, because you have found favour with me, and I know you by name (Exodus 33:17, NEB).

FAITH IS A RESPONSE, reacting to prior causes and events; it is the acceptance of certain things and the rejection of others.

Moses moved from the valley of perplexity to the mountain of certainty, and he did it by faith, not by sight. God would not allow him to "see" his full glory, but what he did allow him to see was so sufficient that God could say, "I have done what you asked," and Moses was so overwhelmed that he "bowed his head toward the earth, and worshipped" (Exodus 34:8).

What was this faith responding to? What were the prior causes and events that enabled Moses to accept fully the testimony of God? What are the sources for any man's faith?

In the prologue of Maxwell Anderson's *Joan of Lorraine*, Masters reviews the fact that, "when Joan was nineteen years old, after she'd crowned her king and saved France, she was captured by her enemies and put on trial for her life. And they asked her the toughest question ever put to the human race: Why do you believe what you believe?"

Why *do* men believe what they believe? There is surely a definitive "getting place" for faith somewhere. There must be common source-norms which men can recognize as authentic causes for the result and response known as faith. Whether it be religion as ancient as Moses' or as new as tomorrow's, there are fundamental reasons, materials, and processes which bring any person to say, "This I believe."

The source-norms for all religious faith, any religious faith, are basically three: the scriptures which a group holds to be sacred, the interpretation and witness of the community of faith through the ages, and the personal experience which one feels he has had in the divine-human encounter.

No faith is complete and balanced without the essential ingredients of all three sources—the scriptural record, the community witness, and the personal experience. If one is omitted or overstressed, a normative religious faith gives way to an abnormal expression. If all three are kept in proper tension with each other, a recognizable and representative faith will emerge.

It is rather easy to see how this threefold pattern

applies to the developing faith of a modern man, but it also applies to the primitive faith of the great Moses. Without theological formulae and ecclesiastical organization, he still had to hammer out his faith from the available materials of the sacred records, the witness from the community of Israel, and his own personal encounters with God.

Upon closer inspection, we can see that this pattern is precisely what God offered as the "given" to Moses when he asked to see his glory. He had said, "I will do this thing that you have asked"; that is, he would reveal as much of himself as he knew Moses needed for faith and fellowship. He then proceeded to name three ways in which he would reveal himself: "I will make all my goodness pass before you, and I will pronounce in your hearing the name Jehovah. I will be gracious to whom I will be gracious, and will have compassion on whom I will have compassion."

The sacred record would be open for Moses' inspection and instruction when God made all his goodness pass before him.

The community witness would add its testimony as God exercised both his sovereignty and his grace in bestowing his compassion upon those of his choice.

The personal experience would happen when God pronounced his private and holy name in the ear of sinful man.

Every man must still travel this three-lane highway to a faith of his own, and a comparison of our journey with that of the ancient traveler may help us arrive at our desired destination. The signs along our way are the same signs that guided him. Sometimes the signs may be difficult to read, but "God is his own interpreter, and he will make it plain."

THE SIGN OF
HIS PASSING GOODNESS

In the Jewish and Christian religions, history and faith are inseparable.

When God tells Moses that he will cause his goodness to pass before him, it is more than a philosophical statement about the nature of God. It is the illumination of the footprints of God across the pages of history. Even the "goodness statement" of chapter 34, verse 6, is couched in the context of historical happenings. The sign of God's passing goodness is to be translated in the language of God's mighty acts in history.

The philosophical religions of the Greeks and Romans were immersed in speculative theories about the unseen spirit world. These tended toward myths and legends, with the gods absorbed in their own activities, uninvolved with the real world of men. The Judeo-Christian witness is based on historical events rather than speculation, and God is always and everywhere involved in the affairs of men.

The primitive religions of uncivilized man have always been concerned with the occurrence and meaning of natural events. They seek for the religious significance of earthquakes, volcanoes, and tidal waves, seeing man and his gods at the mercy of nature. The biblical God, on the contrary, is the Creator and Controller of nature, and even man has been commissioned to have dominion over the earth.

The mystical religions of the oriental world are absorbed with the concept of direct involvement in spiritual ultimates, without the need for mediation between deity and humanity. Their basic premise is the total oneness of the universe. In the Jewish and Christian traditions, the God of revelation allows himself to be known by man through chosen channels of mediation, the primary vehicle being that of history.

Christian theology is developed almost exclusively on the historical account of a man called Jesus of Nazareth, seeing him as the culmination of the historical faith of Israel. In fact, Christians will take a step further into historical faith than even their Jewish forefathers have gone. They will place the dimension of personal experience into the historical past. Even though the Jew will speak reverently of the Exodus as the central historical act of God, he will never say that his personal salvation depends on it. But that is precisely what the Christian does say when he speaks of the crucifixion-resurrection event of Jesus Christ: that there and nowhere else is his salvation accomplished.

Although the Moslem recognizes the Hegira, the flight of Muhammed to Mecca, as the decisive and sacred event of history, he would never think of saying that Allah was reconciling *him* by that event. Yet the Christian's central message is that God was in Christ, reconciling the world unto himself.

Without hesitation and without apology, the Christian acknowledges that his faith is a historical faith, grounded in the passing goodness of God. Our Scriptures, both Old and New Testaments, are products of history and history is their subject. The first source-norm for a viable faith is the sacred scriptures of any religion. Since the Jewish and Christian Scriptures are basically historical, they parallel with the "passing goodness" which God promised to show Moses.

The objection arises, however, that Moses did not have a scripture such as we have, and it may seem artificial to compare God's passing goodness to our scriptural source-norm for faith. But the point is that the passing goodness that God showed Moses is what in fact became an integral part of our sacred Scriptures. We read it in a biblical text, and Moses received it in a divine revelation, but it is the same message, the mighty acts of a gracious God in the history of men.

A great portion of these mighty acts which comprised the passing goodness of God were preserved within the tribal oral traditions which had been carefully passed down from the days of the patriarchs: Abraham, Isaac, and Jacob. The Joseph stories had been given special veneration and protection as symbolic of God's providential care for his people. In every instance of God's dealing with the patriarchs, he is seen in a loving posture which gives credibility to the idea of his passing goodness.

Another portion of God's mighty acts which would eventually be included in Moses' records came from the primeval traditions which included the creation account, the flood story, the sagas of the mighty men before Abraham. Although wickedness and faithlessness were dutifully recorded, every time God intervenes he is the God of righteousness and justice. His work is always characterized as a passing goodness.

The greater portion of God's mighty acts which would become sacred both to Moses and to us came from his own personal observation of God's dealings with his people. It included the Exodus and the events at Sinai, the building of the tabernacle and the institution of Jehovah worship, the faithless cowardice at Kadesh-barnea and the subsequent wilderness wanderings, the reconstruction of the nation and preparation for the conquest of the promised land. The negative was preserved with the positive, and evil was reported along with good. But every time God is obeyed and honored, the results are positive and good. The human part of the story contains both sin and holiness, but the divine part always features the passing goodness of God.

This distinction is essential if we are to understand properly the meaning of revelation through history. If all of history reveals some facet of God at work, then we are stuck with the age-old problem of explaining how a righteous God can perform evil acts.

On the other hand, if we see history as revealing God
at work among men who retain their free choice to do
or reject God's will, we can more easily distinguish
the footprints of God from those of men.

The evil in the world comes not from God, but
from men who have rejected God. In fact, it would
be a greater evil on God's part if he did not allow the
evil on man's part to reap its natural harvest. God
stands in the midst of history, calling men to a broth-
erhood of love in which they do not kill or steal or
covet or bear false witness. If, therefore, men decide
to live in anarchy, with each following the impulses
of his own emotions and desires, chaos and tragedy
must result. If God is true in his revealed standards
for men, he must remain true in his judgments when
those standards are violated. It would be a monstrous
thing to have pain removed from the world, for then
men would allow themselves to be hacked to pieces
and their children to be starved. Pain and suffering
are God-given signals that something is wrong and
needs to be righted.

Thus Moses comes to know his own history and
the history of his forefathers as the environment in
which God is working to make his message plain. It
is a message of grace and righteousness. It is a message of his passing goodness.

How can I read the signs and interpret the message? What word is from God? Will he always be
found to be just and good, or will he confuse me with
subtle variations of light and dark? The New Testament answer is that "all good giving, every perfect
gift, comes from above, from the Father of the lights

of heaven. With him there is no variation, no play of passing shadows" (James 1:17, NEB).

So, I will read your records, Moses, and those of your colleagues who have joined you in the fifteen-hundred-year venture of compiling the Word of God. Because you and they have so carefully pointed out to me the footprints and fingerprints of God in your history, I will be able to compare them with similar signs in my history.

You asked to see God's glory, Moses, and the first thing he pointed to was the historical record of his righteousness. I want to see his glory also, and I too am finding more and more evidence of his presence as I read carefully the signs of his passing goodness.

THE SIGN OF
HIS GRACE COMMUNITY

The fellowship of God's chosen comprises receivers rather than achievers.

The community most closely identified with biblical faith will be one which recognizes the sovereignty of God and exists because of his grace. The signs that convey ever-increasing knowledge about God seem to consistently come from the community of faith. A people open to God's grace in the first place will be more likely to be open to his revelation in the second place.

The second source-norm for building an authentic faith is the witness of the Christian community through the ages. I cannot arrive at a mature understanding of what God is doing in his world until I have heard the testimony of the church as to what God has done throughout history, and the interpretation the church has given to those acts and messages of God. If I am an honest seeker I will also want to hear how the church has interpreted the Scriptures. If I am a humble believer I will even be willing to let the church speak to and about my own experience. Between the first source of faith—the holy Scriptures—and the third source of faith—my personal experience—I must be willing to consider the second source, the witness of the church.

The sign of the witness of God's people was as vital to Moses' faith as it is to mine. He had asked to see God's glory, and God had replied with the threefold "given," the sign of his passing goodness (historical Scriptures), the sign of his grace community (church witness), and the sign of his given name (personal experience). The second sign related to a serious need in the development of Moses' faith.

Earlier Moses had insisted that he and Israel needed the presence of God to assure them that he had chosen them. He also expressed a growing concern that the rest of the world should recognize Israel as a distinct people, set apart for God's purpose in the world. He was identifying himself with a community of faith.

If ever a man had legitimate claim to a personal, exclusive religion, it was Moses, who had so many personal encounters with God. He would not, however, get by on the laurels of his individual piety or personal calling. He never divorced himself from the people called Israel. His purpose was theirs, his destiny was theirs. After the tragic apostasy in which the people reveled while Moses was receiving the commandments, Moses prayed for God to forgive the people, and if he could not, to blot out his own name also (Exodus 32:32).

Later, in Exodus 34:9, Moses again prayed for God
to forgive the people, but he used the first person
plural, identifying himself with sinful Israel: "And
pardon *our* iniquity and *our* sin, and take *us* for thine
inheritance." When the Israelites later heard of the
"giants" in the land of Canaan, they murmured
against Moses and God, and the Lord told Moses he
was ready to disinherit them all and start over with
him (Moses) to build a new nation. Rather than being
exalted by such a signal honor, Moses was deeply
distressed over the negative witness this would give
the world, and interceded successfully again for God
to spare his people (Numbers 14:11-21).

Every time Moses had the opportunity to leave the
community and strike out on his own, he rejected the
notion and took his stand with God's people, whatever the outcome might be. He knew that real religion is not to be discovered in isolation, and that we
become authentic persons only as we take our place
in the family of God.

With such a community-consciousness, Moses
would also understand that any revelation given to
him was not just for his own personal enjoyment or
enrichment. He was to be a vessel, through which
God could communicate. He was not the end-object
of God's grace, but the intermediate-channel. This
one self-concept kept Israel alive. If Moses had ever
seen himself as the most important, the final recipient
of God's will, the whole enterprise would have fallen
apart. No community of faith can survive when
members start seeing themselves as recipients rather
than channels of God's blessings.

Yet the very thing that keeps us in the role of

channels is the realization that we have received. We
are recipients *in* the line, not at the end of the line.
"Freely ye have received, freely give." Those who see
themselves as having achieved their status, whether
physical or spiritual, will insist that others must
achieve also. Those who know that everything, even
faith, is a gift of God, are more able to understand
giving and sharing with others. A genuine grace community reflects not only the grace of God to man,
but also the grace of man to man.

The sign of God's grace community was expressed
thus to Moses: "I will be gracious to whom I will be
gracious, and will show mercy on whom I will show
mercy." The sovereignty of God culminates in his
grace, and his grace justifies his sovereignty.

If I hear God saying only that he will do what he
wants to do, I can conceive of a God who is self-cen-
tered and unsympathetic to the plight of oppressed
men. I can also imagine that he is unapproachable,
without any disposition to let me in on his plans.

If I hear God saying only that he will show mercy
and grace, I may be tempted to ask if he is able to do
it. I may feel that he is sincere but just not capable of
that much power.

But if I hear him say that he can and will do what
he wants to do, and that what he wants to do is show
grace and mercy, then I have a God who is not only
disposed toward mercy, but is also capable of accom-
plishing it. He is a sovereign God, all-powerful, and
he is a God of grace, all-merciful. Both of these as-
pects of his nature are illuminated in the superlative
presentation of Christ in John 1:14 as "full of grace
and truth."

The sovereignty of God includes will as well as power. He not only has the power to do; he also has the prerogative to choose what he will do. Further, he not only chooses to show grace and mercy; he also chooses those upon whom he will bestow grace and mercy. Therefore, the second sign he promised Moses is not simply a society of human beings, but a particular kind of community, a grace community.

A grace community does not create itself; it is called into being by the spirit of God. A grace community does not need to produce credentials for its validity; it knows itself to be an authentic part of God's family. The grace community does not strive for unity and organization; it literally flows with harmony and orderliness. A grace community has no reason to fear competition or hostility; it is promoted and protected by the omnipotent God. A grace community is not anxious about success or survival; it knows that its only true success is the glory of God, and that it will exist as long as God needs it for that purpose. A grace community comes from God, lives for God, and yields to God. It is, therefore, a reliable sign of God's presence and manifest glory in his world.

The world has always had its grace community for a witness to the living God. Out of his grace, God created man and made him the focal point and beloved favorite of Eden's splendor. When man degenerated into sinful rebellion, God, in his sovereign grace, elected Noah and his family to salvage mankind and receive the covenant of the bow. The idolatrous civilization of Mesopotamia caused God to elect Abraham and begin the long migration away from polytheism to monotheism. The patriarchal covenant was passed to Abraham's son and grandson as the election process continued. Moses was elected for the role of deliverer, Joshua as conqueror, Saul as the first king, and David as the consummate expression of God's elective purpose.

The idea of election by God's sovereign grace was deeply imbedded in Israel's history and theology. Yet without the Exodus event, there would have been no substance or credibility to the idea of divine election. At the Exodus, the people of Israel learned indelibly that God was more powerful than the greatest temporal ruler of the age, even Pharaoh himself. They learned that he could control and command the forces of nature to serve him. They learned that for some unknown reason he had shown his pity upon this poor defenseless people and had chosen them for himself.

They were a people now, and although God would continue the election of individuals for leadership, it would be through the people as a whole that he would bless the earth. They were chosen as vessels of God's grace to the rest of the world.

This doctrine of election which permeates to the heart of all Judaism was not born in speculation. It evolved from the interpretation of definite historical events. Also, the election of God was never seen as based on human power or righteousness. Israel is often represented as being hardhearted and rebellious, even after the miraculous delivery from Egypt.

Then why had God chosen Israel? The only answer is that election is rooted in the mystery of divine grace. It cannot be explained; it can only be accepted in faith and gratitude.

Is it fair that God should choose some and not others? The only possible answer is another question: Is it possible for God to be unfair? He who is all-wise, all-knowing, all-powerful, all-loving, all-righteous surely bestows his grace and exercises his sovereignty in absolute equity and rightness.

Questioning God's justice in the business of election is not a new chapter in biblical criticism. Centuries ago, the Apostle Paul dealt with this knotty problem in all its ramifications, and used for his Old Testament text the very words which God spoke to Moses that day on Sinai. "A word of promise came to Rebecca, at the time when she was pregnant with two children by the one man, Isaac our forefather. It came before the children were born or had done anything good or bad, plainly showing that God's act of choice has nothing to do with achievements, but is entirely a matter of his will. . . . Now do we conclude that God is unjust? Never! For God says long ago to Moses: I will have mercy on whom I have mercy, and I will have compassion on whom I have compassion. It is obviously not a question of human will or human effort, but of divine mercy" (Romans 9:10-16, Phillips).

Thousands of years this side of Moses men still contend about the worthiness of a doctrine of election, and they still perplex themselves with trying to figure out the complex system of how God does it. Yet such anxiety is not necessary for us who now have his word on the matter.

The ultimate election of God's grace was completed in Christ Jesus. He is now the Elected One, and all those who accept and believe him share in his election. "He hath chosen us *in him*" and we can speak of our election only in the sense that it is his; we share it only because "he hath made us accepted in the beloved" (Ephesians 1:4, 6).

The grace community exists because of the grace of God, in the grace of God, and for the grace of God. As his community it hears him and speaks for him; it receives him and shares him. As his community it obeys and honors him; it worships and witnesses to him.

The grace community cannot call itself nor save itself. Neither can it call or save the world by itself. It can only give what it has received and the only thing it has is what it has received. The only reason for its being is to serve as an extension, a voice, a sign of the sovereign grace of God.

If I discover a community of faith which is of God's grace, I have found another sign to heed carefully as I continue searching to see the glory of God. God walks with his people, and if I look in earnest for his footprints, I will need to look where his people have walked.

THE SIGN OF
HIS GIVEN NAME

When a name is given, a self is shared and a relationship has begun.

In our Western culture a person's name is primarily
a preferred means of identification. For some it simply indicates that John is not Bob. For others it lo-
cates an individual within a particular family, and
most names reveal the person's national or ethnic ori-
gin. We share our names with new acquaintances so
that we will know what to call each other. Sometimes
we drop our original name and assume another's, as
in the case of marriage or adoption. The basic purpose in all of this still remains that of identification,
the singling out of one person from all others.

It is thus extremely difficult for us to understand
the intensity of the importance of names in the Scriptures. For the Hebrews, a name stood for far more
than identification. It denoted the character of the in-

dividual; it was the verbal embodiment of his character. The name always expressed the totality of a person; it was not a label attached to a body, but the essence of one's wholeness in mind, body, and spirit. To attack or defame one's name was to assault his entire personhood. To take God's name in vain was to engage the whole concept of God in spurious unreality, to question his very existence or importance.

To pray in Jesus' name means infinitely more than tacking a verbal formula onto the end of a prayer. It means approaching God in the very spirit, attitude, intentions, desires, and will of Christ himself. To stand before God in Christ's name is to stand before him in Christ himself. To believe on his name means to be submerged totally and trustingly into the nature and person and work of Christ himself. "A name above every name" refers not simply to fame or honor, but indicates the ultimate majesty of the total person of Christ.

It is a shame that Christians, who incidentally are called that because they bear his name, should have lost the significance of names in the culture in which their faith began. The New Testament echoes the vibrations of the name-encounters of the Old Testament, but twenty centuries later they have almost faded into obscurity. We will not understand what is really happening with Moses, and with us, until we hear it in the biblical value tones of the sacred name.

The third source-norm for developing a mature faith is personal experience, and the most vivid way in which God could have communicated the validity of a personal experience to Moses was to give him his

name, the very essence of himself. When Moses
asked to see God's glory, God replied, "I will make
all my goodness pass before you, and I will pronounce in your hearing the Name JEHOVAH" (Exodus 33:19, NEB). In ancient times, the giving of a
name was an intimate and trusting act. It meant a
willingness to expose who and what a person was. It
included the disclosure of background, family, position, and character. It made the person open and vulnerable, for once his name was known he could be
encumbered or ensnared by the adverse use of his
name. Of course, he could also be enhanced and en-
nobled by the proper use of his name. In a very real
sense, to know someone's name put the knower in the
position to control that person.

These same name attributes applied to gods as well
as to men. The tribes and nations of men had been
eager and quick to name their gods, for thus they
could control them. They could limit them to be
gods of the day or gods of the night. By an explicit
name, one god would be allowed to control the elements, another the crops, another the wars, another
fertility, etc. In fact, by sacrifice and ritual the wor-
shipers could determine how much control the god
had. The secret was to know the god's name and call
upon the correct god to accomplish the desired action.

The God of the Israelites never allowed himself to
be placed in the pantheon of man-made gods. He
would not even allow his name to be known in the
early days of Israel's development. He was referred
to simply by the general term for deity, pronounced

in the Hebrew as *El* or *Elohim* for the plural form: "In the beginning *Elohim* created the heaven and the earth." Occasionally he might be referred to as *El-Shaddai*, the Almighty One (or mountain god). In Genesis 33:20, Jacob "erected there an altar, and called it *El-elohe-Israel* [the God of Israel]."

It was not until Moses stood before the burning bush that the proper name for God was revealed. When God told him that he wanted him to be the deliverer that should bring Israel out of Egypt, Moses replied, "'If I go to the Israelites and tell them that the God of their forefathers has sent me to them, and they ask me his name, what shall I say?' God answered, 'I AM; that is who I am. Tell them that I AM has sent you to them.' And God said further, 'You must tell the Israelites this, that it is JEHOVAH the God of their forefathers, the God of Abraham, the God of Isaac, the God of Jacob, who has sent you to them. This is my name for ever; this is my title in every generation. Go and assemble the elders of Israel and tell them that JEHOVAH the God of their forefathers, the God of Abraham, Isaac and Jacob, has appeared to you'" (Exodus 3:13-16, NEB).

At last the Israelites had a name for their God. But if he was the same God of the patriarchs, didn't they know his name? No, not the name revealed at the burning bush. Later, in Egypt, when God encouraged the discouraged Moses, he explicitly told him that he had made a new disclosure of himself to Moses that even the patriarchs had not known: "God spoke to Moses and said, 'I am the Lord. I appeared to Abraham, Isaac, and Jacob as God Almighty [*El-Shaddai*]. But I did not let myself be known to them by my name JEHOVAH'" (Exodus 6:2,3, NEB).

The name *Jehovah* was not the actual name given in the original Hebrew of the Old Testament. It was a name coined in the sixteenth century by Christian theologians, combining the vowels of *Adhonai* (Lord) with the consonants of JHVH, producing the form Jehovah which has been retained in nearly all translations since that time. The letters JHVH were derived from the original Hebrew consonants JHWH, the name pronounced to Moses by God. The original text of the Old Testament was without vowels, and when these are added from the word *Adhonai* to JHWH, the closest we can probably get to the pronunciation of the name that Moses heard was *Jahweh* (which our English Bibles call Jehovah).

Jahweh is an expanded form of the Hebrew verb "to be," and means not only absolute existence, but also "he that is present." To Moses, God said that he was "Jahweh, I Am That I Am." He was the self-existent One, the uncaused, unconditioned, self-sufficient, all-powerful. The name also implied, "I will be what I will be, and I will do what I will do."

This is the name, and therefore, the essence of the character and person of God as revealed to Moses on Sinai at the burning bush before Moses went to Egypt to free his people. Why, then, was God now telling Moses that in response to his request to see God's glory, one of the things he would do would be to pronounce his name in Moses' presence? Hadn't he already done that?

The answer to that question can be found only in the fulfilling of the promise itself. The next day God took Moses back up the mountain and did pass before him and pronounce his name Jehovah; but in the pronouncing of it, he elaborated into an account of what the name really revealed about God. "And the Lord came down in the cloud and took his place beside him and pronounced the Name JEHOVAH. Then the Lord passed in front of him and called aloud, 'JEHOVAH, the LORD, a god compassionate and gracious, long-suffering, ever constant and true, maintaining constancy to thousands, forgiving iniquity, rebellion, and sin, and not sweeping the guilty clean away'" (Exodus 34:5-7, NEB).

The former revelation at the burning bush had established God as self-existent and self-sufficient, and the subsequent events of the Exodus had confirmed his power, freedom, supremacy, and changelessness. But nothing had specifically testified about the moral attributes of Israel's God. The fact that he was all possible perfection implied the presence of moral attributes, but that had not yet been declared by divine revelation.

In this descriptive declaration of his nature, God revealed that he was a God of mercy, truth, and justice. There is the accumulation of terms that are nearly all synonymous: Merciful, gracious, long-suffering, abundant in goodness, keeping mercy for thousands, forgiving iniquity and sin. It is the expanded expression of that definitive testimony which should come from John's pen centuries later, beautifully and simply stated, "God is love" (1 John 4:8).

Once and for all, Israel now knew not only the name of her God, but also his nature. He had revealed himself, exposed himself, and as it were, made himself vulnerable to them. Now they could profane his name, take it in vain, and shame his name before the heathen nations. But they could also bless his name, hallow it, and proclaim it among the nations. They had a choice, and a responsibility, to respond to the given Name.

To compare my personal religious experience with the name-giving experience of Moses involves more than a simple statement that I believe in the name of Jesus Christ, the Son of God. It involves appropriating for myself the same two meanings of the name Jehovah as given in the encounter between God and Moses.

First and foremost, God repeated to Moses the identical name that he had pronounced at the burning bush. Moses could not comprehend the nature of God unless he really believed in the existence of God. For a true knowledge of God, I must, first and foremost, have the conviction that there is a self-existent Being, eternal, uncaused, the cause of all things (and therefore of my own existence), on whom I am absolutely dependent. It is only after this that I may inquire and learn the moral character of God.

An authentic Christian experience or encounter with God has not occurred until the second meaning of his name, the moral character, has become a personal part of my faith. I become a Christian not simply by believing that there is a God, but by trusting him to be a loving, merciful, just, and forgiving God.

To him I can confess and repent of my sins. From him I can expect forgiveness and reconciliation. To make this possible he has given himself in the person of his Son, even as he gave himself to Moses in the pronouncing of his name. The giving is of itself testimony to the nature of his love. It is essential to the being of grace or love that it manifest itself. *Love unrevealed is love unreal.*

Like Moses I have sought to see the glory of God, and like Moses I have found abundant evidence of that glory. I have seen his passing goodness, in the Scripture-history of my faith. I have heard the witness of his grace community in the fellowship of his church. I have received his given name in the personal experience of repentance and faith.

God has blessed me with plain signs to read that point to himself. But a sign is only a sign; it always points beyond itself. The Scriptures are not God; the church is not God; personal experience is not God. They all point to God, but in the pointing they cast a strong shadow that looks remarkably like the back of God.

THREE
In the Cleft of the Rock

He hideth my soul in the cleft of the rock
That shadows a dry, thirsty land;
He hideth my soul in the depths of His love,
And covers me there with His hand.

from the hymn
He Hideth My Soul
by Fanny J. Crosby

The Lord said, "Here is a place beside me. Take your stand on the rock and when my glory passes by, I will put you in a crevice of the rock and cover you with my hand until I have passed by" (Exodus 33:21, 22, NEB).

PRESENT OBEDIENCE is the best recommendation for future responsibility.

Until one has proved that he can be a follower himself, he has not qualified to lead others. Preparation to receive greater blessings begins in grateful acceptance of the present gifts. How can we recognize God's glory when we see it unless we obey his voice when we hear it?

God had told Moses of three signs which he would give him, all pointing to the glory of God Moses had asked to see. Moses was willing to accept and eager to read the signs. Since he did not reject the signs or ar-

gue that they were insufficient, God was ready to
move him on to the next plateau of preparation.

The first plateau is the acceptance of the given
signs which become the source-norms for structuring
our theology, or building our faith. The second plateau is the assuming of a posture toward God's
world. The first plateau involved concepts and experiences: Scripture-history, community witness,
and personal experience. The second plateau involves
the created physical world in which these concepts
and experiences are received.

If I want God to reveal his glory to me in this
world, I must assume a posture in and toward this
world that will make it possible for me to receive his
glory. It is a world that I did not create, but inherited. There are physical laws as well as spiritual
which I must acknowledge. How can I hope to become spiritually knowledgeable if I insist on remaining physically ignorant? If I cannot honor God with
what I see, how can I honor him with what I cannot
see? I cannot hope to be master of much until I have
learned to be faithful in little.

Moses was required to position himself in a definite way before God would lead him to the next step
of revelation. If I follow humbly I may also be able to
learn the posture and the place where God bids me
stand.

STANDING WITH GOD

The Lord said, "Here is a place beside me. Take your stand on the rock."

The rock was physical, tangible, of this world, and in this world. It could be seen, weighed, and measured. It was created by the same God who had created Moses, and each shared a common atmosphere and location. Unlike Moses, however, it had no soul, no mind, and no ability to choose its destiny. If it ever became more than an inanimate object gathering the dust of the ages, it would be by the will of God or the hand of man. It might become "a mighty rock in a weary land" casting its shadow for the weary traveler. It could become part of a wall or foundation of a palace. It could be broken into pieces and become dangerous weapons.

At this time and in this place, the rock was for Moses a place to stand. By thus standing he affirmed

the presence and strength of the rock to support him.
He acknowledged his own need of something concrete on which to take his stand. He identified himself as a physical being in a physical world.

Moses discovered that when he obeyed God and
stood where God told him, he was not alone; God
himself was with him: "Here is a place beside me."
God had never asked him to go anywhere alone. Just
as surely as Jahweh meant "I am that I am," it also
meant, "I will be where I will be." Not an inch of
God's created world exists without his power and
presence. Regardless of where God bids us go, it is
never a sending-away-from but a calling-to his presence. If he bids me stand on a barren rock on a lonely
hill in the back side of the desert of Sinai, I can be
sure that he is beside me.

Standing with God on the rock is symbolic of my
posture of acceptance of God's created world. The
rock may not be a color or texture that I prefer, but it
is the one I am told to stand upon and it is where
God has promised to stand beside me. The world
into which I have been born may not be exactly as I
would create my ideal world, but it is the one I have
been called to live in and where God has promised to
be with me.

There are those who say they will believe in God
if he will change the world to suit them. There are
others who believe in God in spite of the world's im-
perfections. They have taken their stand with God
on a bare and lonely rock when they might have preferred a lush and fragrant garden. Those who wait
until conditions are ideal to believe never understand
the glory that is unveiled by the back of God.

The true believer does not believe in God *because* he performs a requested deed. He believes in God *regardless* of deeds and events. When Nebuchadnezzar condemned Shadrach, Meshach, and Abednego to the fiery furnace, they replied, "If it be so, our God whom we serve is able to deliver us from the burning fiery furnace, and he will deliver us out of thy hand, O king. *But if not*, be it known unto thee, O king, that we will not serve thy gods, nor worship the golden image which thou hast set up" (Daniel 3:17, 18).

This is real faith, to believe that God can control the physical elements of the fire which he has created, but to remain true to him regardless of what he does. God does not have to keep proving himself in repeated acts of power to the true believer.

There are many today whose praise of God has grown silent on their lips because he did not perpetuate their happiness or protect their loved one or preserve their world. No man has suffered greater loss of all these things than the stricken Job, who looked up from the ashes of his misery to sing, "The Lord gave, and the Lord hath taken away; blessed be the name of the Lord" (Job 1:21).

I sat through a long night of waiting at the hospital with a young couple who feared that every breath of their precious child might be her last. Prayers were answered, the child survived, and the grateful parents came to see me the next day to rededicate their lives, saying that now they knew God was a God of love. I rejoiced with them, but gently reminded them that God would still be a God of love even if their child had not lived. To place our whole faith and

dedication on one gracious act of God is at best a
very tenuous relation with the Almighty Creator and
Sustainer of the universe and its millions of inhabi-
tants.

If we must have a physical miracle in order to believe, one miracle should be enough, the miracle of
the incarnation, the miracle of John 1:14, "The Word
became flesh and dwelt among us, and we beheld his
glory, the glory as of the only begotten of the Father,
full of grace and truth." No man since then should
ever need proof of God's existence, or power, or love.
If the obstacles and problems of this world cause me
to doubt the presence of God with me on this rock, I
have only to turn to the life of Jesus Christ to be reminded that "this is my Father's world, and though
the wrong seem oft so strong, God is the ruler yet."

Some travel a darkened road of pain and cry out
daily that God should show himself strong and merciful in their behalf. The Apostle Paul thus prayed,
beseeching God three different times to remove his
"thorn in the flesh." Paul said that God told him,
"My grace is sufficient for thee: for my strength is
made perfect in weakness. Most gladly therefore will
I rather glory in my infirmities, that the power of
Christ may rest upon me" (2 Corinthians 12:9). Not
only was he willing to accept this crude rock of a
world where he was required to stand, he praised
God that it gave him a chance to be the channel of
God's grace.

When Isaac Watts wrote his immortal hymn, "Am
I A Soldier of the Cross?" he exclaimed in the third
stanza one of the most profound insights a man has

ever had: "Is this vile world a friend to grace, to help
me on to God?" When a soul ceases to curse the im-
perfections of the world and the weaknesses of the
flesh, and begins to see them as vehicles bearing him
closer to trusting God, he is developing a posture toward this world that will allow him a glimpse into
the next.

The contours of the back of God begin to take
a clearer shape as I learn to focus my eyes of faith to
see his image even among the rocks and deserts of my
life. I know now that I cannot expect him to give me
further revelation of himself unless I am ready to
stand beside him against a hostile, taunting world
and affirm in the words of Job, "Though he slay me,
yet will I trust him" (Job 13:15).

SHELTERED IN THE ROCK

Provisions unused are no better than provisions unknown.

The man who can read and doesn't is no wiser than the man who can't read. The sick man who refuses to use the medicine at hand will get well no sooner than the native who has never even heard of medical science. One of man's noblest attributes is the ability to discern the provisions which nature has supplied for his welfare; and one of his most unproductive attitudes is the rejection or waste or abuse of those provisions.

When God prepared Moses to receive the revelation encounter he had requested, he placed him in a crevice of the rock nearby. This may have been a small cave in the side of Mount Sinai. The twofold significance of the cleft or cave was its provision in the first place, and then Moses' willingness to avail

himself of its protecting walls. He did not question
the necessity for hiding in a cleft rock; he assumed
that God knew what he was doing. Neither did he
question the safety or reliability of this particular
cave; again he trusted God's wisdom and timing.
This was the place where Moses was at the time of
the encounter. There may have been more comfortable caves elsewhere, but for this time and this place,
Moses was instructed to use what was at hand.

We cannot understand and translate the "back
of God" until we are sensitive and open to providential provisions in this life which are reflections of
God's presence. That image of God for which we are
constantly reaching will keep eluding us until we
open our receptivity centers to the daily signals
which he is trying to send us through our existing
supplies.

We conclude that primitive civilizations were here
before us when we discover their artifacts and buried
cities. We can trace their vocational pursuits and so-
cial mores by the archeological evidence. Just as con-
clusively we can trace the footprints of God across
his universe as we uncover evidence of the divine
presence.

How is that evidence verified as being of God? By
consistency. If the God who revealed his nature in
the pronouncing of his name is a God of mercy,
truth, and justice, the evidence of his presence will
testify to these traits. If God is merciful and protective, he will provide a cave for Moses at the right
place and time to meet his needs. Those natural supplies provided providentially for man will be con-

structive, not destructive; they will preserve and protect and enrich man's existence.

Man, however, will not always avail himself of those provisions, or he may pervert them to ungodly uses, and they will become destructive forces. But this is the perversion of man, not the provision of God. It was God who placed the iron ore in the earth for man's provision, but it is man who decides whether he will make a sword or a plow with the iron. If man ignores the belching warning of the volcano and builds his village too close to the mountain, he cannot accuse God of being evil or unprotective when the lava flows down.

The provisions of God will be consistent with his nature: mercy, truth, and justice. When the provisions appear as otherwise they have either been misunderstood or misused by man. The back of God may not reveal the features of his face, but it will not be contrary to it. We may not be able to know everything about God, but that which we do know bears the stamp of God in his mercy and truth and justice.

In his disposition of love toward man, God provides that which he needs, sometimes centuries before it is needed or discovered. The rock which sheltered Moses had been there for hundreds, perhaps thousands, of years. The crevice had split the rock, forming a sliver of a cave, ages before Moses would need it for just one afternoon.

Wallace Hamilton once wrote, "Think how the Creator has waited long centuries of time for the mind of man to open, to break through, and to learn

even a little about the hidden mystery of creation.
All these powerful energies here—these here-before-
we-got-here things—half-concealed, waiting for
someone's seeing eye and hearing ear." Emerson once
hinted that they could have had electricity in the
Garden of Eden. It was here from the beginning of
time, waiting.

Uranium has been here all along, hidden in the
rocks, to be discovered and utilized only in this, the
nuclear age. Thousands of years before man began to
use them, coal and oil existed in abundance. Nature
had been storing up man's cellar with fire and fuel for
his use, but for generations he shivered in his cold,
damp houses, not knowing what was under his feet.
Who knows what vast secrets of the universe are yet
unlocked, what provisions of God are yet undiscov-
ered?

In his autobiography *From Pagan to Christian*, Lin
Yutang said, "If I were God, and therefore a master
chemist and physicist, I would be extremely interested in seeing how the chemists and astronomers
and biologists on earth proceed to unlock my secrets.
I would, of course, remain silent and give no help.
But I would be very interested in watching their discoveries, giving them perhaps a century or two to
pry open my secrets and think them over and work
them out."

Does one have to be a scientist to discover God's
provisions? Are there special locations in the earth
where one must go to pry open his secrets? Not at
all. As Joseph Henry, the American physicist, said,
"The seeds of great discoveries are constantly floating

around us, but they only take root in minds well prepared to receive them."

This, then, is the key to opening the doors of providential provisions; a mind prepared to receive them!
A mind and attitude that expect great and good
things from a great and good God. A mind that
thinks God is a provider who knows well in advance
our needs. A mind that is capable of seeing the parallel between the physical world and the spiritual
world, because the former is but the shadow of the
latter. A mind and heart and soul that are willing to
penetrate deeply into the essential nature of this created world, and into the attributes of the God who
created it and ordained the nature of its laws.

If I hope to move closer to the back of God
and touch the hem of his garment, I must wake up to
the world in which he is walking and working, and,
indeed, has been walking and working since time im-
memorial.

If I cannot see God in the splitting of the rock to
provide a shelter for Moses, I will not likely see him
in the formations of nature in my world. If I cannot
acknowledge the wise and loving concern of God in
storing up fuel for the physical needs of man, I will
have a hard time identifying the hidden resources for
spiritual energy. If I believe that my world is here
only by chance and natural evolution, without a divine mind and purpose behind it, I will never be
completely sure that God is in control of anything.

On the other hand, I may have already begun to
unravel a part of the mystery about the back of
God when I am able to sing from my soul:

*This is my Father's world,
And to my list'ning ears,
All nature sings, and round me rings
The music of the spheres.
This is my Father's world,
I rest me in the thought
Of rocks and trees, of skies and seas;
His hand the wonders wrought.*

COVERED WITH HIS HAND

The silence of God may be the most eloquent testimony of his presence.

His hand touches your eyelids and they are closed to the light. His hand holds your arms and you are not able to perform as you planned. His hand restrains your feet and you cannot go where you wish. His hand covers you and you are shielded from the view you had hoped to see. His hand touches your lips and others' and his own and silence drops its curtain across your world.

Your first instinct is to cry out against the silence and the darkness and the restraining hand. If there is a God, why doesn't he "do" something, meaning, of course, why doesn't he let you see what you want to see, go where you want to go, do what you want to do, and say and hear the words your heart craves?

Surely the "glory" of God, the presence, weight,

and substance of God can best be known and felt
when aggressive action is being expressed and allowed. Not necessarily. In fact, the strongest evidence that God is with us may be the very restraint
he has placed upon us.

When God told Moses that he was going to place
him in a crevice in the rock and cover him with his
hand, Moses may have felt a momentary rejection of
the idea. Wouldn't this be a rather awkward position
for a prophet who had come to the mountain to see
God? How could he participate in the grand event of
revelation if he were stuck in a hole and God's hand
were holding him there? How could Israel's leader
take them to the promised land if he couldn't even
get himself out of the rock? How would he be able to
see and hear God when he passed with this impene-
trable "hand" covering him?

Yet it was the very thing that seemed an obstacle
that turned out to be Moses' only hope of being
God's man. The force that kept him in that rock sheltered his eyes from the blinding brightness of God's
presence. By restraining him, God's hand prevented
his impatient plunging into the arena of revelation
before God was ready for him. By covering him
gently, God kept him from hurtling blindly down the
craggy slopes to danger and death. God perhaps
never proved his presence so clearly to Moses as in
that moment when he covered him with his hand and
seemingly closed Moses off from all that was happening outside.

This momentary restraint and cover was probably
a vivid reminder to Moses of the long silent years in

the back side of the desert. He had already learned that men who are chosen to lead must be disciplined to wait. He had been shut off from the worldly affairs of men. Reared as Pharaoh's son, educated and talented, born to be a leader of men, he had ended up leading his father-in-law's sheep. God's hand had covered and held him back for forty years.

Now that great hand was covering him again, saying, "Wait a moment, Moses. You have waited before. You can wait again. I'll let you out of the rock when I am ready."

How many times have I strained against the hand of God, trying to move it just enough so I could inch my way out of this barren rock? How often have I felt that God was unreasonable to expect me to do great things for him but wouldn't turn me loose? How bitterly have I resented the fact that others were allowed to be out there where God is while I was shut up alone with him and that immovable hand of his?

Then there came the quiet but growing realization that it was God's will keeping me there, and that he wills only what is best for me. Perhaps the closed door which kept me from fulfilling my ambition also kept me from entering a nightmare of heartaches. Perhaps the guide who forced my stubborn feet down a path other than the one I had chosen knew of deadly dangers that lurked in that way. Perhaps the confinement of this crevice in this limited rock is the safest place on earth for me at this time.

And the darkness that moves in when his hand overshadows. That, too, I am learning may be a sweet

provision of his tender care. If I saw too much too
soon, I might rush impetuously into foolish activity. I
might tell too much too carelessly of the sacred
things of God. I might chase to and fro in the excite-
ment of bright revelation without taking time to
think and pray and grow inwardly as only the darkness inspires a man to do. I might also selfishly forget
the millions who still hover in physical and spiritual
darkness, waiting the touch of one who cares and
knows what it's like in the dark.

And the silence that prevails when his hand shuts
me off from the rest of his activity: that, too, may be
the surest sign of his presence and wisdom. He
knows I need to learn to exist as a child away from
his father. He knows that constant fathering is not
the best way to mature a child, that too much de-
pendence stifles growth.

A constant sound soon loses its impact and indi-
viduality. It becomes an expected part of the rest of
the background noises of life. Its urgency and authority are diminished if it drones on and on. If a familiar voice has something to say about every single
issue and every minute item it may not be heard
when the big issues need to be spoken to.

Incessant instruction may also imply that the par-
ent or teacher does not yet trust the child to make his
own decisions. God's silence in my life may mean
that he thinks I am growing up and can handle this
situation. He may be standing silently in the wings
like a proud father watching his child perform as he
has taught him.

I need to know God's presence, power, and love in

my life every minute of every day. But this does not mean that I have to have him hovering over me, telling me what clothes to wear, helping me with my grades in school, and whispering directions in my ear at every intersection.

In fact, I may not qualify for that fuller revelation of his "glory" until I have been able to accept without fear and frustration the seeming silence and darkness and restraint of his covering hand. Moses was thoroughly satisfied with the back of God when it was revealed to him because he had already learned to be satisfied with whatever God gave him or kept from him.

Some bright day we will thank God for the love that covered us and restrained us, but even now we can testify that:

> *We walk by faith and not by sight:*
> *No gracious words we hear*
> *From him who spake as man ne'er spake,*
> *But we believe him near.*
>
> *We may not touch his hands and side,*
> *Nor follow where he trod;*
> *But in his promise we rejoice,*
> *And cry, My Lord and God!*
>
> *Help then, O Lord, our unbelief!*
>
> *And may our faith abound*
> *To call on thee when thou art near,*
> *And seek where thou art found:*

That, when our life of faith is done,
In realms of clearer light
We may behold thee as thou art,
With full and endless sight.

FOUR
Hid from Our Eyes

Immortal, invisible God only wise,
In light inaccessible hid from our eyes.
All praise we would render; O help us to see
'Tis only the splendor of light hideth Thee!

from the hymn
Immortal, Invisible
by Walter Chalmers Smith

Then I will take away my hand, and you shall see my back;
but my face shall not be seen (Exodus 33:23, RSV).

WHEN THE MOMENT OF TRUTH finally comes in our
lives, we discover that the real issue is not the event,
but our response to it.

We wait and pray, yearn and search, dream and
plan, and finally the decisive day arrives. All our to-
morrows seem to hinge on this one pivot of our lives.
In days to come we will look back and say that this
was the turning point. But if we would reflect clearly
and objectively about it, we might recall that "the big
event" wasn't really all that big. In fact, it might even
seem to be written in a minor key compared to some
of the other orchestrations of our lives.

Then it might dawn on us that the actual turning
point, the real moment of truth, was happening in-

side us. We were finally reaching a place in our maturing process that enabled us to take a stand, or make a decision, or handle a difficult situation in such a decisive way that we felt we had turned a significant corner in our journey. It was not what happened *to* us that mattered, but what happened *in* us. The big chance we've been waiting for may appear in the form of the big change that comes from us.

God had been showing himself strong in Israel's behalf for a long time. His call to Abraham had echoed across the Mesopotamian valley five hundred years before. Even Moses had seen spectacular upheavals of nature testify to the awesome power of God. In fact, the incident between God and Moses on Sinai that day might seem almost a trifle in comparison with other displays of divine grandeur. Indeed, few people are even aware of the events in Exodus 33 and 34.

The momentous part of the occasion was that Moses was finally ready to receive whatever God had to reveal. He had boldly asked to see God's glory, but he would ask no more. He would accept God's answer and be satisfied with it until the end of his days.

This spirit of absolute trust and surrendered allegiance can make the ordinary events of any day turn into a once-in-a-lifetime moment of truth. When we are truly ready to receive, we will find that God has been waiting, ready to give what we need of himself.

HIS HAND REMOVED

Openness makes us both resilient and vulnerable.

The hand of God had covered Moses in the cleft of the rock, providing protection, silence, and darkness. While that was the safest place for the moment, it would soon have become a destructive place for Moses. Too much protection causes the body to atrophy, to weaken and wither away.

The human body, like a plant of the forest, needs sunshine, wind, and rain to grow. It needs to climb hills and lift weights to strengthen its muscles. It can never be strong and resilient against the elements if it remains in protective isolation.

Do not stay too long in your little cave, Moses. You may grow to depend on it, even to like it. You could learn to fear anything outside, even the light— especially the light. The protecting hand of God is to be appropriated and appreciated, but if you continue to demand it for your own welfare, you could miss out on the bigger world outside.

Like Moses, if I am to experience a more meaningful encounter with God, I must be willing to let him remove his hand at the right time in order to reveal the rest of him. There comes a time when I have to step out of the confining crib in the nursery and explore the rest of the house, and someday the neighborhood.

I surely will learn eventually that when God removes his hand, I do not need to conclude that he no longer is or that he no longer cares. Rather, I will know that he cares about my freedom and growth too much to keep me caged forever. He exposes me to the winds of the wilderness that he might more vividly expose himself to me.

There is danger in it, though. When I stand open on the hillside I am vulnerable to nature's whims and the beasts of the wilderness. I will have to learn to shield myself against both attack and neglect. Sometimes out in the open world there will be too much pulling and probing at me. Other times there will be too few who even know I exist. It will be alternately too crowded and too lonely, and hardly ever just right.

There will be sunlight that brightens and illumines my path, but sometimes it will grow too bright and dazzle my eyes. It will play tricks on my vision and make me see things that are not really there, even false images of God.

There will be darkness that protects and ushers in

sweet peace, but sometimes it will be filled with strange sounds and darker memories. It may remind me of that peaceful darkness in the cave, but it may also remind me of that outer darkness where there is never peace.

There is security in the cave of memories as we dwell on what God has done. But there is insecurity on the open mountainside as we gaze on what God is *doing*. One day in a moment of truth I will have to decide whether to retreat into the security of what God has done or plunge into the insecurity of what he is doing.

For, sooner or later, God will remove his hand. In a way suited for each individual, God will let it be known that he is ready to move on with us to greater knowledge of his person and will. He may seem to take a long time before he brings us to that cross-roads, but he will. God may take his time, but he is never late.

Someday each person will receive his opportunity to step out and up into a new and fuller relationship with God. He will face the choice of staying where he is or going where God is. God only removes his hand. He does not forcibly pull us out of the rock. That is our task and our decision, to come out or stay there.

Leonard Griffith says so provocatively, "The biggest obstacle to Christian belief does not lie in some thorny theological issue, nor yet in some burning practical issue, but in our own timidity and indecisiveness. If we are not Christians, it is not because

our religious questions remain unanswered, but because we cannot reach a decision, we cannot make up
our minds to follow Jesus Christ."

He then reminds us of the parable which the Dan-
ish theologian Kierkegaard told about a flock of geese
that milled around a filthy barnyard, imprisoned by a
high wooden fence. One day a preaching goose came
into their midst. He stood on an old crate and ad-
monished the geese for being content with this con-
fined, earthbound existence. He recounted the ex-
ploits of their forefathers who spread their wings and
flew the trackless wastes of the sky. He spoke of the
goodness of the Creator who had given geese the urge
to migrate and the wings to fly. This pleased the
geese. They nodded their heads and marveled at
these things and applauded the eloquence of the
preaching goose. All this they did. But one thing
they never did; they did not fly. They went back to
their waiting dinner, for the corn was good and the
barnyard secure.

But could things ever be the same again? Once
they knew it could be different, would they be satisfied and feel as secure as before? What would have
happened to Moses if he had stayed cowering in the
crevice? Would the hand of God have returned to
shelter him still? Or does God remove his hand and
leave us with our decision? If that is the case,
wouldn't we be better off meeting whatever encounter out in the open?

The time has come. Moses' prayer is about to be
answered. God has prepared him and protected him
for this hour. Now it is all up to Moses. He must ac-

cept whatever God has to show him. His moment of truth has arrived, but so has he. His spiritual development has kept pace with his increasing opportunities, and he is ready for the next word from the Lord.

HIS BACK UNVEILED

Those who are able to recognize each piece of the puzzle and put it in its proper place will not be surprised nor disappointed when they see the completed picture.

Moses had attentively followed God step by step to arrive at this moment of revelation. He had started by being honest about his own limitations and needs: his desire to know God's ways more fully, his need to know that he belonged, and the basic cry of his soul for positive proof, asking plainly to see God's glory.

Then he accepted and read intelligently the signs God gave him: his passing goodness in the history of mankind, his sovereign grace in the gathered community, and the personal experience of his given name.

From there Moses took his place beside God. He accepted the natural provision of the rock's shelter;

he acknowledged the need for God's protecting hand; and he left the crevice when the hand was removed.

Looking out from the small cave, he saw evidence of the image of the Creator of the universe, an image so clearly God's and yet so unclearly defined that the only description which seemed to fit was that of *the back of God.*

At last, after eighty long years, he was standing before the form of God, but what he saw was not the face but the *back* of his beloved "Jahweh." Yet Moses did not groan or complain that the revelation was unfair or not enough. His lack of disappointment may indicate that Moses was not terribly surprised, that this fuller revelation of God's back was just a clearer picture of what he had already accepted as God's nature and activity. Although the view from the back does not present distinctive features, it does give a contoured outline of a recognizable silhouette. Moses recognized the silhouette of God against the vast sky of the Sinai wilderness because he had already touched the outline of God in the contours of previous experience.

In "the hidden depths of many a heart" the outline of God is already taking shape in the yearning and searching and praying. The desire to know God was placed there by God himself and is testimony to his nature, a God who wants fellowship with his creatures. My craving to know more, my need to know I belong, and my request to see his glory are all footprints across my soul that tell me he has walked quietly here, hoping I would follow.

The promise that "he will make it plain" features

the overt expression of his activity. Whereas my inner searching gives a subjective witness to his presence, an objective witness is given by the recorded facts of history, the life of the church, and the personal experience of millions. There is something of God in each sign, not enough to be complete by itself, but forming a distinguishable outline of deity when synchronized with the other signs, which beckon and point the way to him.

"In the cleft of the rock," I have come even closer to God. Daring to take my stand for God by faith without sight, I have felt the stirring of his strength beside me. Accepting the provisions for necessity as gifts he has left behind, I have felt the warmth of a caring love. Yielding to the resulting conditions of his overshadowing hand, I have sensed his peace and purpose in circumstances beyond my control.

Having come this far in faith and having felt God's presence so often, Moses would have been surprised if he had not discovered God outside that crevice, and he would probably have been surprised to have seen anything but his back. It was the shadow of God's back he had been working with all along, so it was the clear outline of his back that he would most readily recognize. God grant that I, too, may recognize his presence anywhere by remembering the signs everywhere.

The signs, however, are always written in the past tense, and perhaps this is the most accurate translation of that strange description of the back of God. Does it mean that we never see God coming, we only see him going?

Kierkegaard said that life must be lived forward, but it is only understood backward. Expanding on this idea, W. B. J. Martin said, "We are always wise after the event. While the event is still proceeding, we are unaware of what is going on. Only after we reflect upon it does it strike us that God was in it all along."

This understanding of *revelation in retrospect* should serve as a balancing factor and a maturing influence in an unstable religious climate that clamors for immediate knowledge of God and his ways. Too many people today want to understand what they have never lived through. They seem to think they have a foolproof theology without even tracking the footprints of God. As Dr. Martin says, "Theology, after all, is looking at God's back, interpreting where he has been in our lives."

Those who are waiting for a face-to-face encounter with God would be spending their time more productively by reflecting on past encounters in their lives. There is where they are likely to find God. Those seeking a religious experience should be looking for the religious message in experiences they have already had.

But wouldn't our faith be more complete and authentic if we could have that one great personal visitation? I'm not so sure, for even the disciples who walked personally with Jesus of Nazareth never fully comprehended who he was and what he was doing. It was after his crucifixion and resurrection that they began to reflect and remember and recall every word, and put it all together. It took them at least thirty years to come up with the first gospel, and then thirty or forty more years to round out the others, adding other remembrances, interpreting this act or that parable, relating the Christ event to the Old Testament, projecting it into the future, turning it inside out, weighing it, measuring it, reliving it, and concluding with unshakable faith that "God was in Christ, reconciling the world unto himself."

The significant insight into that statement of faith is that they didn't know it themselves when it was happening. They discovered this basic Christian affirmation by revelation in retrospect. It takes most of us nearly a lifetime to learn this process.

I have been a Christian for almost forty years. I have been consciously and actively studying or proclaiming the Christian message nearly every day of that forty years. I have had many personal excursions into the pilgrimage of faith. I have bowed in the valley of despair and I have sung on the mountain of hope. I have been excessively blessed by the touch of Christian love from countless hearts. In my spiritual quest, I have asked and received, I have sought and found, I have knocked and had doors opened.

I am a Christian by conversion, conviction, and commitment. I believe that "the Word was made flesh and dwelt among us" and that in this incarnation "God was in Christ, reconciling the world unto himself." The longer I live and the more I study and preach the Christian message, the stronger I believe it, and the more real God becomes to me.

Now, with that kind of lifetime involvement and commitment, you would think that I would never have any problem recognizing God. Surely by now I ought to be able to identify the One who has been my constant companion and the object of my life's devotion these many years.

Yet the harder I strain to see him through earth-bound fog, the clearer it becomes to me that all I am seeing is his back side. I have had enough experiences which I do not hesitate to call divine encounters to think that I can identify him even if it is only his back I see. In my more certain moods I am ready to call out to him and have him turn around so that I can introduce you to him. When I fantasize about this happening, I see him greet me affectionately and then smile warmly at you and say, "I'm so glad to meet you. Any friend of Bill's is a friend of mine." All the time I am standing aside, smugly smiling as though to say, "See, I told you I knew the Almighty."

But just as I am about to bring this off, that enor-mous back moves and that giant arm reaches in a way that is new and strange to me. Just when I think I know all of God's moves, he strikes out in a new flurry of activity and leaves me bewildered. Just when I think I have traced his footprints in the sands of history, I stumble across a whole continent of revelation I have never seen. Just when I think I have mastered his doings and meanings in the Holy Scrip-tures, I am humbled as a kindergarten child staring dumbly at complex equations.

God will not let me box him in. He insists upon his freedom to be God. His ways sometimes are not my ways, and his thoughts are surely above my thoughts. As a child I was able to recognize him by familiar patterns of action. Sometimes now it seems that I recognize him most quickly by unfamiliar, unexpected movements. I am more and more convinced that "God moves in mysterious ways, his wonders to perform."

Yes, it is intellectually stimulating and spiritually invigorating to think that I stand with the great Moses when I gaze intently at that mighty back of God. But it is that very presence which causes me some of my most complicated problems. Yet the problems may providentially be used by the Spirit of God to help me more clearly identify the contours of that majestic silhouette.

If I cannot identify God irrevocably by his actions in nature and history, perhaps I should allow him the sovereignty to work where and how he pleases, and thereby increase my opportunity to see him more often.

If I cannot identify God permanently in any given culture or style, perhaps I should be flexible enough to expect God to show up anywhere, and thereby heighten my anticipation of his coming.

If I cannot identify God categorically as belonging with any certain kind of people, perhaps I should look for his image in every face I meet, and thereby multiply the relationships of love and joy in my spiritual journey.

If I cannot identify God in these spurious, trivial, external ways, perhaps I can learn to "be still and know that he is God."

Elton Trueblood was conducting a seminar in one

of our local churches which my wife and I attended.
I wrote my master's thesis on Trueblood's doctrine of
the laity and he became a supportive friend, personally and professionally, through the years. Every
time I hear him speak, or visit with him personally,
he comes up with a novel approach to an old problem.

In the local seminar he was fielding questions from
the small core group when he again graced us with a
fresh directness. A man who was trying to decide
about entering politics asked Dr. Trueblood when a
person could know beyond the shadow of a doubt
what God's will was for his life.

Without hesitating, Trueblood said bluntly but
kindly, "You never can."

There was an audible gasp from the audience as
though he had uttered an obscene word in the sanctuary. We have been taught all our lives to learn and
do the will of God. We have heard dedicated
Christians, young and old, speak dogmatically about
knowing the will of God. We have made countless
decisions ourselves on the basis of believing this was
God's will for our lives. Then this venerable prophet
of church renewal takes our breath away by saying
we can never know for sure.

After allowing us to recover from the shock of his
almost-sacrilegious pronouncement, he proceeded to
discuss thoroughly and carefully the process we all
follow in trying to know God's will. He reminded us
that we pray and study God's Word, that we seek the
counsel of wisdom and experience, that we recall the
lessons learned from previous decisions, that we com-

pare and contrast and judge, and that finally we conclude that we know what God wants us to do. We
act on that conclusion and later we are sometimes
certain that we were right; sometimes we feel that we
were wrong; and many times, we just don't know.
Our growing understanding of God's nature and will
is nearly always related to past experiences of faith-
judgments. This is revelation by retrospect, this is
learning to live with the back of God.

But what about that clear message and that unmistakable conviction that it is God who spoke the message? Surely man is capable of knowing when God
has spoken to him. The answer is both yes and no,
and the experience of Moses again provides the context for the paradoxical answer.

At the burning bush on Sinai God talked directly
to Moses, telling him to go to Egypt and deliver the
Israelites from bondage. "'But who am I,' Moses said
to God, 'that I should go to Pharaoh, and that I
should bring the Israelites out of Egypt?'

"God answered, 'I am with you. This shall be *the
proof* that it is I who have sent you: when you have
brought the people out of Egypt, you shall all worship God here on this mountain'" (Exodus 3:11, 12,
NEB).

Moses knew that there was a God and that he was
communicating with him. He had great difficulty,
however, in understanding the divine directions, and
especially his part in them. God realized Moses'
problem and told him that he would give *historical
confirmation* to the message. When you stand on this
mountain again, Moses, and all the liberated Israel-

ites are gathered with you to worship Jahweh, then
you will have your *proof* that it really was God that
day talking to you out of the burning bush!

Not even a mysterious burning bush is enough;
not even a supernatural voice from heaven is enough.
The authenticity of the message was to be verified by
the fulfillment of definite promises. History itself
would reveal that it was God who had spoken. If this
is essential for Moses' faith process, how much more
so for those of us who have never seen burning
bushes or heard heavenly voices?

This, then, appears to be the Moses pattern which
should also be mine: Because of what I know about
God in past actions, I can believe that the message I
am receiving is from him, but even that message will
need confirmation by historical events yet to happen.
My feelings are not enough, my dreams and desires
are not enough; my prayers and intuitions are not
enough. I must not declare authority short of the
footprints of God in time and history. I can say with
assurance that it was God who led me after I have
seen the evidence of his leading.

I must be open but humble about direct inspira-
tion. I must honestly say, "Upon the best understanding I have of God and his Word, in the experiences of prayer and the presence of the Holy Spirit,
utilizing the witness of history and the counsel of
godly persons, I believe that this present decision is
the will and way of Almighty God. However, I cannot know this positively and absolutely until I have
seen the promise fulfilled, and have traced the footprints of God in the developing events. Until then I

must reserve the right and responsibility of acknowledging that my feelings were wrong. The back
of God is all that I am ever given to see, and even
that much of him can be seen only in retrospect."

In a climate of overzealous religion, we may feel
intimidated to speak with less than dogmatic certainty. We might be made to feel that we have little
faith or no faith at all. We could even lose some posture of leadership, for the crowds flock to a person
who claims to speak the last, authoritative word of
God. Men do not normally like to be told that they
must think and weigh and judge, and especially do
they dislike having to admit they made a mistake.

It will probably never be popular to tell men that
they will have to settle for the back of God.
Some people will not accept the fact that they personally will never be shown the face of God in this
life. But Moses accepted it for himself. He had asked
to see God's glory, and was shown his back instead.
He knew once and for all that he would have to follow this God by faith and not by sight. And with
this faith he brought the children of God to the
promised land.

HIS FACE UNSEEN

Refusing an unwise request is often a father's clearest expression of love.

God had told Moses that he would let him see his back, "but my face shall not be seen." This was the second time he had made that point. The first time came immediately after he disclosed the signs he would give to Moses: "But he added, 'My face you cannot see [and this time he told him why], for no mortal man may see me and live'" (Exodus 33:20, NEB).

In case Moses may have thought God refused to show his face because Moses was unworthy or God was uncaring, the loving Father explained that it was his own concern for his child's welfare that demanded a lack of full disclosure. It was unselfish love expressed in merciful mystery. If God were to allow

Moses to see his face, rather than blessing his servant, it would destroy him.

Why can't a man live after beholding the face of God? Is it because the receptors of the human brain are not adequate to receive the infinite expressions and impressions that would focus together in the assimilating of all that is God in one place and one time? The sheer force of that impact would surely short-circuit the nervous system, bombard the mind with more unknown factors than it could equate, and explode the heart in a rushing tide of emotions. Neurologically and psychologically no man could survive the assault that a vision of the total essence of God would make upon him.

But is physical danger the only reason for caution against asking to see God? Could sinful man tolerate the weight of guilt that would descend upon him if he saw the purity and loveliness of God? Would he will himself to die in a desperate attempt to escape those eyes of absolute righteousness and justice?

God, however, is a forgiving God of compassion and reconciliation. If we saw him as he really is we would instantly know that he loves and forgives. Perhaps the sheer joy in being with such a Heavenly Father would motivate us to seek release from this life that we might hurry to share eternity with him. Is it possible that men would just refuse to live once they had seen a glimpse of what it would mean to behold his face forever? Could we ever go back to things as usual after knowing ultimate beauty and perfection?

Whatever our speculations might be about the rea-

sons and means for the destruction of man upon
seeing God, it is quite plain that God intends to
make a serious point with this bit of information.
Man cannot have both earth and heaven. He cannot
gaze upon the face of God and continue to live normally among men. He cannot handle the mysteries of
the Creator as long as he occupies the body of the
creature.

Some would choose the heavenly over the earthly
and the vision over life. But God does not give us the
choice on this one. He has already decided that even
the great Moses will not be allowed to decide. God
knows every man better than he knows himself, and
he has decreed (not offered) that no man shall see him
in his full disclosure in this life. Those who claim to
have seen the fullness of God have taken unto themselves a privilege that is not sanctioned and autho-
rized by God, but is in fact in direct opposition to his
expressed will.

The tragedy is that men would trade the mercy of
God for the secret to his mystery. They would rather
have knowledge than love, and experience instead of
faith. They seem not to have heard God say that the
reason he cannot and will not reveal and explain
everything to them is because he loves them too
much.

In his infinite wisdom and love, my Heavenly
Father knows exactly how much I need to know, and
he keeps from me that which would confuse or
weaken or destroy. I must continue to seek, but always be ready to accept what I find. I must try to
understand God better and love him deeper, but I

must not expect ever in this life to know and see all there is of God. He loves me too much to let that happen.

Even as I pray serenely and believingly, I have to admit that restless thoughts keep rolling around underneath the surface of my calm communication with God. I feel very close to Moses at this point. In his searching encounter with God he seemed to be carrying on a very calm and orderly dialogue with the Lord. He was telling God what he needed, and God was reassuring him that he understood. Each issue was being discussed and dealt with in a straightforward and seemingly satisfactory manner. Moses appeared to have all his requests in a neat package and God appeared to be satisfying those requests, one by one.

Then suddenly Moses exploded, "Show me thy glory!" Obviously, the great man of faith was not as calm and assured underneath as the surface conversation had implied. Like a volcano building up over the years, the ultimate request erupted before Moses could stop it.

"Show me thy glory! Just let me see you plainly, clearly so that I will never doubt again. Make yourself known and seen in an objective reality, not in my own subjective feelings or religious philosophy. If you will only stand here before me in some unquestionable revelation of your person, all of the communication problems will be over. My questioning and doubting and worrying will cease. Your use of multiple vehicles and instruments to communicate to me will not be needed any longer. If I could have just

one moment of face-to-face encounter, you and I
would understand each other from then
on . . .wouldn't we?"

Yes, I know how Moses felt, and if I were on as
intimate terms with God as he was, I would probably be crying (demanding, perhaps?) that God show
me his tangible glory. The desire to see God is not an
effort to halt all communication with him. On the
contrary, it is a yearning to open up better and
brighter avenues of communication. I want to look
into God's face and hear his words clearly and distinctly from his own lips, not through some preacher
or printed page or historical event.

Lord, why do we have to keep talking to you
through fogs and mists and cloudy skies? Why do we
need to keep searching for ways to get through to
you, with prayers and music and art, with architec-
ture and crusades and achievements, with thinking
and preaching and writing? Wouldn't it be much sim-
pler to speak with you in a mutual language what we
feel and dream and desire?

Why, also, Lord, do you continue to address us
from unexpected locations, with obscure messages
delivered in changing code styles? Why are we left
with so much responsibility to decode, translate, interpret, and respond to your message? Wouldn't your
will be accomplished so much quicker and surer if
you just faced us directly and told us what you expect, and what we can expect?

As I understand it, this is what Moses wanted,
too, but he did not get the full measure of his request. God told him ways in which he would com-

municate with him, but the face-to-face meeting was impossible. He would have to do business with the back of God.

And so will I. He will talk with me, and he invites me to talk with him always about everything, but he will not turn around. This means that I may sometimes wonder if he has heard me. I will not be able to see a facial expression that acknowledges he has heard. I may not hear or see any particular demonstration of an answer to my words. I may have to leave my words at his feet, believing in faith that he will respond in the grace and wisdom that are his alone.

If he keeps his back to me, I will not be able to tell whether he is smiling or frowning, or even weeping. I will have to learn to judge the pleasure and displeasure of God by other methods than a look into his face. I may even have to learn an appreciation for the experience of others who have been listening to his voice longer than I, or the freshness of new believers who have not let the message become dull with repetition and boredom. It is possible that I may learn to read the "body language" of God, seeing a message in his mighty acts among men rather than hearing an audible voice in my ear. I am already positive of this one thing, that what I see him do will always correspond with what I hear him say. He will never contradict himself. His communication may not always be clear to me, but it will always be true to himself.

Communication may be a problem as I face the back of God, but it may also be potentially dynamic, growing and becoming more fulfilling with

every encounter and every word. I must listen more
carefully to get the message clearly, and I must think
through my own words more diligently so I will
know exactly what it is that I want to say to God.
Above all, I must keep the channels open and the
dialogue flowing. Just because the pilot cannot see
the air traffic controller in the tower, he does not
switch off the receiver and transmitter and attempt to
land on his own. The voice from the tower could
very well represent the signal I keep getting from
God: "I know you can't see me, but don't worry, I
can see you. I know where you are and what you
need to do. Keep the channel open. Keep talking,
keep listening. I'll bring you home safe."

God was not through with Moses. Revelation is
not the end but the beginning of service. We do not
ask to see God in order to cease working for him, but
on the contrary, in order to work better for him.

Although his face is unseen by Moses (and us), his
work is not unseen and unknown. The glory of God
we have asked to see may be waiting in the vineyard
to which he has called us.

FIVE
For the Living of These Days

Set our feet on lofty places,
Armored with all Christ-like graces.
Free our hearts to work and praise,
For the living of these days.

from the hymn
God of Grace and God of Glory
by Harry Emerson Fosdick

Be ready by morning. Then in the morning go up Mount Sinai; stand and wait for me there on the top (Exodus 34:2, NEB).

THE REAL GLORY OF GOD is not a momentary flash of sensational brilliance; it is the continuing life style of an abiding relationship.

If, therefore, we are serious in our request to see the glory of God, we had better be ready to live with it for the rest of our lives. God does not play games of hide and seek, here today and gone tomorrow. Neither does he burn brightly for a moment like a holiday sparkler, and then leave us with a still, dark night.

God is constant and consistent; he is durable and dependable. He is the same yesterday, today, and forever. The God who spoke to Moses on Sinai was

the same God who spoke through Christ on the
Mount of Olives, and he is the same who speaks to us
today.

After God had disclosed the nature of the signs he
would give, and the method of revealing his image,
he told Moses to meet him the next morning on the
mountain. We should not cry out impatiently to see
God unless we are willing to prepare ourselves for
the meeting, climb up to where he is, and wait for
him at the top.

The most essential prerequisite, however, is the
readiness to accept the lifelong changes that will
come from the encounter. We cannot expect to return
to business as usual once we have felt the breath of
God. Neither can we hope to have one moment of
splendor and then live in its afterglow. His invitation
is to follow forever, with no turning back.

Then the glory we have sought, the true glory of
God, will become obvious in the everyday events of
our lives. It will manifest itself in various but definite
ways. It will still be featured as the back of God,
a shadowy outline which is definitely there but dimly
seen.

Yet we will know that this is the glory of God. We
will know because we have recognized our deepest
needs, we have read the given signs, we have accepted the providential provisions, and we have
known the unseen face and the unveiled back.

Now we will live the rest of our days in the glory
(the presence, weight, and substance) of God who
knows just exactly how much of that glory we need
"for the living of these days."

NEGATIVE GLORY IN CLOSED PATHS

God often reveals most clearly what he is like by tell-ing us what he doesn't want us to be like.

In a cherished moment of serious dialogue with our son, I asked him how he had found God most frequently revealing his will to him. In profound simplicity he said, "Dad, I'm not always sure what God wants me to do, but I'm nearly always positive what he doesn't want me to do. So when I try to eliminate from my life those things I know are wrong, it seems that all of the big issues about God's will somehow get settled also."

The presence of God, which is what Moses called the glory of God, may sometimes be best identified as a negative glory. That which God is *not*, suggests what God *is*. Also, there is a negative aspect to the will of God when he closes certain paths to us. By knowing where he does *not* want us to go, we can

more accurately determine where he *does* want us to
go.

In the last verse of Exodus 33, God said to Moses,
"You shall see my back; but my face shall not be
seen." In the very next verse, which is the first verse
of chapter 34 (and a continuation of the same conversation), he said, "Cut two tables of stone like the first;
and I will write upon the tables the words that were
on the first tables, which you broke" (RSV). Then he
told him to meet him at the top of the mountain the
next morning.

God's commandments are as much a part of his
self-revelation as his creation. Through the creative
product that is nature we can know of the power and
majesty of God. It is through his commandments,
however, that we learn about his moral values and
concerns.

If Moses was to see an adequate vision of God he
would have to take the tables of commandments into
account. Every time he etched a figure in the stone,
another facet of God was etched in his own heart.
With every requirement for the creature, he learned
something else about the Creator.

When the commandments were as complete as
they needed to be, Moses would be able to step back
and look upon the stones, and perhaps he would
imagine that he saw the shape of the stone tables as
the outline of a man's back, for once again he had
discovered another representative of the back of
God.

On the other side of every commandment is the

face of God. When I understand what this side is all
about, I will realize better what that side must be
like. How can I hope to comprehend his countenance
on that side when I have not been able to comply
with his commandments on this side?

The commandments of God are not simply prohibitions upon man's liberty. They are vivid tools of
revelation to allow us a clearer picture of the God we
worship and serve. In the first place, the very fact
that he cares enough about the welfare and happiness
of the creature to provide him with guidelines for a
meaningful life is "exhibit A" for an immanent God,
compassionately involved with man.

When God says, "Thou shalt not kill," he is not
only preserving the existence and dignity of individuals. He is revealing that he is a God of life, the Creator and Sustainer of life, one who loves life and
wants every man to enjoy it fully. His only begotten
Son would one day say it plainly, "I am come that
they might have life, and that they might have it
more abundantly."

When God says, "Thou shalt not commit
adultery," he is not arbitrarily forbidding pleasure
and emotional relationships. He is telling us that he
is a God of integrity and faithfulness, unwavering
and dependable. He is expressing his concern for the
preservation of the family, for the care of the children, the fidelity of the parents. He is showing that
he wants to rid the home of guilt and shame, of broken promises and broken hearts.

When God says, "Remember the Sabbath day, to

keep it holy," he is not trying to tie men down to a trivial religious observance. He is demonstrating his concern for the physical refreshment and spiritual devotion which man needs to be a whole person. Jesus amplified this unselfish concern of God for man when he said, "The Sabbath was made for man and not man for the Sabbath."

The commandments of God should be seen, therefore, as his negative glory. By closing paths of danger and destruction, he opens highways of peace and joy. It is true that there are things God does not want us to do, but in defining those negative things, he gives us a positive view of himself.

The laws of God were not given for religious ritual, nor for devotional study alone. They are not just handy tools for memory work in Bible class. Neither do they constitute a secret talisman to protect one from harm.

God's commandments express the desire of his eternal heart for his creature, man. In a very real sense, they are the summons of God, his call to the soul of man. God has taken the initiative, he has spoken first. He has revealed himself. He has told us what he expects of us. Now he waits for our response.

The commandments could just as easily have been posed as questions: "Will you have no other gods before you?" "Will you make no graven image?" "Will you refrain from taking my name in vain?" While it is true that in their original form, they are explicit declaratory edicts, they still imply a response. Every law of the land requires a decision-response. The traffic sign which bears only the word "Stop" is actually asking the motorist, "Will you stop?" A decision must be made, one either obeys or disobeys, and response validates or cancels the authority of the command in each life.

It is not really a question of "keeping" or "breaking" the commandments. It is a question of negative or positive response. Am I for them or against them? Will I make these divine imperatives the guide for my life?

The answer we give either opens or closes the possibility of our experiencing the glory of God. If we are not willing to give our affirmation to his expectations, how can we have expectations of further affirmation from him? Why should we hope to have God tell us more about himself when we haven't handled very well that which he has already told us? And we must remember that the commandments are not just prohibitions on man's activities; they are very real instruments of revelation as to the nature of God.

My life now is in an interim state. I have discovered in Scripture, community, and experience what God is like. I believe that that intellectual and spiritual discovery will be confirmed someday when I stand in his presence in the halls of eternity. In the meantime, I am still in this flesh, and need viable vehicles by which I can communicate this faith I am carrying around.

One of the very first vehicles which I must appropriately use is the revelation of God in his stated

standards for our human conduct. As I abide freely
and joyfully by the commandments of God, I will
discover another dimension of the glory of God that
will equip me in this interim, "for the living of these
days."

POSITIVE GLORY
IN NEW HORIZONS

Being able to see where we are going is not nearly as
important as knowing whom we are following.

Thus far in our quest together, you may have been
thinking that this whole idea of the back of God
is a negative concept. You may feel that it is discouraging to be told that we can never see God's face,
that our contact with him will have to be indirect
rather than direct, that revelation is given through
history and nature and reflection. Perhaps you have
seen the negative glory in closed paths as being a
hindrance rather than a help to understanding God
better.

If this is the case, you should be encouraged, perhaps even exhilarated, over the bright promise of
God's glory being discovered in the new horizons to
which he is leading us. His glory is his evident presence, and his presence is never more evident than
when he is leading us up and onward.

After Moses had reviewed the passing goodness of
God and had heard him pronounce his holy name
with all its meaning, he heard God again promise to
lead the people of Israel into the promised land of
Canaan. It would be a rich land, flowing with milk
and honey.

It would be a new kind of land for the people.
They would be transformed from wandering nomads
to farmers and ranchers. They would dwell in cities
and become merchants. They would fight battles and
build kingdoms. They would erect temples and de-
velop an organized religion. Their new land would be
different and they would become different themselves. Following God always involves change. Let
none seek his presence who is determined to remain
the same.

Neither the change nor the challenge is to be
feared. It is the Lord who offers both, and the Lord
who will supply the needs for both. "The Lord said,
'Here and now I make a covenant. In full view of all
your people I will do such miracles as have never
been performed in all the world or in any nation'"
(Exodus 34:10a, NEB).

The new horizons in the different land will witness
these manifest miracles in order to bear testimony to
the power of Israel's God. "All the surrounding
peoples shall see the work of the Lord, for fearful is
that which I will do for you" (Exodus 34:10b). Our
desire to see the glory of God manifested should
never be for our personal welfare only. Our prayer
must always include the concern that the watching
world will be able to see the obvious hand of God at

work. Israel was chosen, not for her own sake, but for the sake of an idolatrous world. The church exists today not for its own sake, but for the sake of a desperately sick world. Our reason for seeking the glory of God must always be that "all the surrounding peoples shall see the work of the Lord."

God's promise of victory in the new land was conditioned upon their keeping the covenant: "Observe all I command you this day; and I for my part will drive out before you the Amorites and the Canaanites and the Hittites and the Perizzites and the Hivites and the Jebusites" (Exodus 34:11, NEB).

To expect God's power without upholding God's holiness is an insult to his justice and to our own integrity. How dare I cry out for God to deliver me from my enemies in the land I go to conquer if I have not delivered myself from the enemies that assault my body and spirit. That which keeps me from doing God's will may also prevent me from entering into promised lands of new horizons.

Neither should I expect the conquering of the new land to be without the cost of battle. It is true that God promised to drive out the various tribes, but he did not allow the Israelites to sit on the sidelines and watch the war games in a giant arena. God did not defeat the enemies *for* them, but *through* them! He wrought the victory for them, but he did it through their swords, their skill, their blood.

There is a price to be paid for every glimpse we get of God's glory. Entrance into the manifest presence of the Almighty does not come cheaply. The holy of holies was made accessible by the price of Calvary's blood. Grace is free, but it is not cheap. He who died for us has the right to expect that we at least should live for him. Only then do we start to see his glory in the new land.

Will it be a face-to-face glory when we enter into new dimensions of faith and victory; or will we still have to do business with the back of God? Of course, it will still be the back of God we see, for we will be yet on earth; but it is a positive and promising perspective. We see his back because he is going before us toward new horizons!

Forty years later, Moses prepared the people to enter Canaan at last. He told them that he would not be able to go with them, but that God had chosen and prepared Joshua to lead them. "And Moses called unto Joshua, and said unto him in the sight of all Israel, Be strong and of a good courage: for thou must go with this people unto the land which the Lord hath sworn unto their fathers to give them; and thou shalt cause them to inherit it. And *the Lord, he it is that doth go before thee*; he will be with thee, he will not fail thee, neither forsake thee: fear not, neither be dismayed" (Deuteronomy 31:7, 8).

Now Joshua would be exposed to the back of God, for as he marched over Jordan and into the central highlands of Palestine he would see that God was going before him, always ahead of him, leading upward and onward.

We have interpreted the back of God in several ways, nearly all of which were related to the past. We have traced his footprints in history, read his signature in Scripture, seen the evidence of his

presence in the community of faith, and heard his
voice speak to our own souls. In all of this, we have
looked back and said in retrospect with Jacob,
"Surely the Lord was in this place."

But we cannot live in the past. We discover our
roots there, but the living exposed branches produce
fruit, not the buried unseen roots. There is a magnetic pull in the universe that draws those branches
upward from the roots and thrusts the fruit outward.
Roots are necessary; however, their purpose is not
mere existence but reproduction.

We are to grow and reproduce the fruits of Christ,
and it must be done in the living present, not the
dead past. The glory of God is to be sought not just
for the assurance of heritage and faith, but for equip-
ping us "for the living of these days." What I believe
because of where I have traced God's presence
should enable me to live as though I am still in his
presence today.

The magnetic pull upward is at work in me even as
it is in nature. I feel and sense and know and respond
to that force of grace that draws me out of the low-
lands to the highlands. The miry clay oozes around
my feet and tries to pull me back into sin, but there
is a stronger power that frees me from its clutches,
sets my feet upon a rock, puts a new song in my
heart, and establishes my goings. (Psalm 40:2, 3.)

This irresistible force is none other than the God
of love himself. He began the drawing venture as the
Father: "I drew them with cords of a man, with
bands of love" (Hosea 11:4). He continued as the
Son: "And I, if I be lifted up from the earth, will

draw all men unto me" (John 12:32). Jesus made it clear, however, that this was the same drawing power of God the Father, not a new or competitive force: "No man can come to me, except the Father which hath sent me draw him" (John 6:44).

This drawing is accomplished through the upward pull. We are able to identify the figure out there ahead of us, even though we see only his back, because he is offering us new horizons, not tying us down to old landmarks. He is offering us new opportunities rather than berating us over past failures. He is challenging us to new conquests, not allowing us to rest on the laurels of past victories.

We can know whether it is God who is leading us when we recognize the pattern we have learned from his past actions. God will not contradict his basic nature, although he may choose different expressions and styles. He will not lead us in paths opposite those in which he led the biblical pilgrims and fellow travelers in the community of faith. We may not know where he is leading, but we can be assured of the ultimate outcome because our God never changes his fundamental direction.

I have no need to fear the new or the unknown; if God is leading me, he has gone before to prepare the way. I need not hesitate at the threshold of a new experience; if God has brought me to it, he will see me through it. I have no reason to doubt the success of the venture ahead; if God has ordained it, he will sustain it.

If I follow after that great moving form of the back of God, I will find that everywhere I go he has

already been. I cannot cross a river without seeing
his deep tracks along the shore. I cannot climb the
steep and rugged mountain without noticing the bent
and scattered foliage where he has surged forward. I
cannot enter into the darkest night without standing
under the stars he placed there centuries before I
came. I cannot swelter under the burning sun without gratitude for shade and breeze he left across my
path.

When I weep, I know that he has wept before me.
When I am hurt and lonely, I know that he was rejected before I was. When I am tempted, I know that
he wrestled the tempter more fiercely than I. When I
am a failure, I know that he saw his work crumble
and his followers fade away. And someday when I
die, I will know that he has also preceded me there
beyond the veil.

"Whither shall I go from thy spirit? or whither
shall I flee from thy presence? If I ascend up into
heaven, thou art there: if I make my bed in hell, behold, thou art there. If I take the wings of the morning, and dwell in the uttermost parts of the sea; even
there shall thy hand lead me, and thy right hand
shall hold me" (Psalm 139:7-10).

He is there when I arrive because he has gone before me. My Canaan is ready for conquering because
he has penetrated its fortresses before me. The one
thing that keeps it from being a strange and hostile
land is that he is already there waiting for me to join
him.

Of course, it is only his back I see. He is always
moving ahead of me, beckoning me to follow. I do

not need him to turn around; I need only to trust and
follow on. It is an active enterprise. It is the positive
glory of God come alive in the gaining of new horizons. It is precisely the hope and promise and activity I must have "for the living of these days."

REFLECTIVE GLORY
IN RADIANT PILGRIMS

The glory we have yearned to see may be so close to
us that others see it before we do.

Moses stayed another forty days and nights on the
mountain, communing with God, and carving out
the commandments on the stone tablets. When he finally came down, Aaron and the Israelites were
afraid to approach him because the skin of his face
shone with a brilliant radiance. Moses was personally
unaware of this strange phenomenon: "He did not
know that the skin of his face shone because he had
been speaking with the Lord." When he realized the
situation, he covered his face with a veil whenever he
appeared before the Israelites, and removed it when
he went before the Lord. (Exodus 34:27-35.)

Although God would not let Moses see his face in
this life, he provided an interim glory "for the living
of these days," until Moses could see God in his full-

ness. Moses was probably not surprised to find God's *negative glory* in the closed paths of the commandments. Nor was he likely to be surprised to find God's *positive glory* in the new horizons of future conquests. But he was caught completely off guard and totally overwhelmed to discover God's *reflective glory* in the radiance of his own shining face.

This is the way with truly great and genuinely humble men. The closer they are to God, the farther they are from self. Moses was entirely unconscious of the difference of his countenance, but bystanders at once noticed it. The ideal radiant life is the one which is naturally so, unconscious of itself.

When David Livingstone came back from Africa, after spending years there for his beloved Africans, someone asked him about his soul. He replied, "My soul, my soul, I almost forgot I had a soul." He was so absorbed in other people's souls that he had almost forgotten about his own soul. To forget ourselves is the most effective way of impressing and ministering to others.

Moses did not deliberately set out to capture a glow that others could see. He was simply absorbed in the work God had bid him do, and he dwelt daily in the presence of God. The glow was not added to him as a reward for his diligence; it was the natural outgrowth of his very life. If I work diligently for God, consciously hoping for that supernatural glow or religious aura, I can be sure that I shall never have it. Moses' formula for producing the radiance was unbroken fellowship with God and unself-conscious plunging into his work. The formula has still not changed.

In fact, Paul used this story about Moses to explain
in vivid detail the Christian's reflective glory in comparison to that ancient episode. Writing to the Corin-
thian church, he said:

*Yet that old system of law that led to death began with
such glory that people could not bear to look at Moses' face.
For as he gave them God's law to obey, his face shone out
with the very glory of God—though the brightness was already fading away. Shall we not expect far greater glory in
these days when the Holy Spirit is giving life? If the plan
that leads to doom was glorious, much more glorious is the
plan that makes men right with God. In fact, that first
glory as it shone from Moses' face is worth nothing at all in
comparison with the overwhelming glory of the new agree-
ment. So if the old system that faded into nothing was full
of heavenly glory, the glory of God's new plan for our salvation is certainly far greater, for it is eternal.*

*Since we know that this new glory will never go away,
we can preach with great boldness, and not as Moses did,
who put a veil over his face so that the Israelis could not see
the glory fade away.*

*Not only Moses' face was veiled, but his people's minds
and understanding were veiled and blinded too. Even now
when the Scripture is read it seems as though Jewish hearts
and minds are covered by a thick veil, because they cannot
see and understand the real meaning of the Scriptures. For
this veil of misunderstanding can be removed only by believing in Christ. Yes, even today when they read Moses' writ-
ings their hearts are blind and they think that obeying the
Ten Commandments is the way to be saved.*

*But whenever anyone turns to the Lord from his sins,
then the veil is taken away. The Lord is the Spirit who gives*

them life, and where he is there is freedom . . . .But we
Christians have no veil over our faces; we can be mirrors
that brightly reflect the glory of the Lord. And as the Spirit
of the Lord works within us, we become more and more like
him (2 Corinthians 3:7-18, The Living Bible).

The privilege is breathtaking, the responsibility is
awesome: "We can be mirrors that brightly reflect
the glory of the Lord!" Think of it; the very glory of
God which men seek the world over to find, they
may find in us. It will not be our glory; it does not
come from us nor reside dormant within us. It is
God's glory and his alone, but he has chosen to reflect it in the lives of his people.

"Christ in you, the hope of glory" (Colossians 1:27)
means for most of us a promise of heaven because of
Christian conversion. But it is more, much more in
the overall dissemination of God's glory. Remembering that "glory" means presence, weight, and substance, we hear the expanding word from Paul saying, "The only hope that God's presence, weight,
and substance can be known and felt in this world is
for Christ to live in and through you." This is reflective and effective glory.

The natural revelation of God in created order
may lead even primitive men to think there must be a
creator. But his loving nature and his redemptive
power are discovered only in the reflected glory of re-
deemed persons. It is there that God has chosen to
reveal the essence of himself. It is there that men discover what God is like by seeing what he wants us to
be like.

When I ask bitterly, "Why doesn't God show me

his glory?" I am chastised by the memory of his radiant presence in the gentle faces of his quiet saints through the years. Nothing can explain the courage and patience and understanding and forgiveness and purity and tenderness which I have seen in noble souls in this pilgrimage of tears except the very presence and glory of God himself. God has shown me his glory in their lives, and it is my mission to continue their witness.

I cannot assume that men will somehow find God in their world; I must show them God in my world. I cannot leave them to speculate on what God should be like; I must reflect what he indeed is like. I cannot excuse myself from witnessing because of spiritual pursuits; the whole purpose for spiritual pursuit is that I may be an effective witness. I cannot decide when I will be God's reflection; I have been so to someone since the day I accepted his grace and took his name.

Yet the remaining paradox is that although I must consciously acknowledge my responsibility to reflect God's glory, I must never consciously seek a supernatural glow to advertise it. It is my part to stay close to God and faithful to my task; it is God's part to equip me with the testimony he deems appropriate.

Where shall I find that presence of God and that appointed task which shall bring his glory to fruition in my life? Not in some faraway places with strange sounding names, but here, where I am, within myself. The Lord Christ told us, "The kingdom of God is within you," and the apostle Paul said that we are "to seek God, and, it might be, touch and find him; though indeed he is not far from each one of us, for

in him we live and move, in him we exist" (Acts
17:27, 28, NEB).

When God inaugurated the existence of man on
earth he began by saying, "Let us make man in our
image and likeness," and the ancient narrator con-
cluded that God did just as he intended: "So God
created man in his own image; in the image of God
he created him; male and female he created them"
(Genesis 1:26, 27, NEB). What was this mysterious
"image of God" in which man was created?

Many scholarly works have attempted to identify
the *imago Dei*, and many devotional works have ap-
pealed to man to discover and fulfill that image. Ar-
guments pro and con have variously discussed
whether the "image" designates the spirit or mind or
personality or will of man. Years ago some even attempted to speak of the physical characteristics of
man as being the image, principally because of the
high anthropomorphism of the biblical material. It is
obvious that no single attribute of man can be iso-
lated as the "image"; and even when we consider man
as a whole, the symbolism is still vague and elusive.

It may be helpful to understand this strange phrase
if we stand again with Moses, viewing the back
of God in his reflective glory. The word used for
"image" is also used for "reflection," the picture of
oneself obtained by looking into a mirror. After mak-
ing all the other creatures of the earth, God seems to
say, "Now, let us make a creature that can reflect the
nature and presence of his Creator, one that can communicate back to God." Thus, the image of God and
the back of God are almost synonymous terms.

We see the "other side of God," the incomplete but meaningful revelation, when we behold his glory in his human creatures.

Dear God, I have been looking for your glory everywhere but have not been still long enough to let it happen in myself. Yes, Lord, I do remember that you said, "Be still and know that I am God," but I'm just beginning to see that you may have implied more than comfort and peace. Were you trying to tell me that I will never truly know your presence, weight, and substance, until I discover in my still, quiet self the reflective glory that is God? That here, in me, is the possibility of "the hope of glory" the world desperately needs? And am I to know all this by the same surrender-experience as Paul: "I am crucified with Christ: nevertheless I live; yet not I, but Christ liveth in me" (Galatians 2:20)?

So the radiance is no cheap bargain-counter cosmetic. It comes at the price of a cross, it lives by dying. Even as Christ Jesus was transfigured before his disciples in a radiant splendor, the subject he discussed with the visiting Moses and Elijah was his impending "exodus" (death) at Jerusalem (Luke 9:28-31). Radiance has a way of being introduced by the somber hues of death. Easter is always preceded by Good Friday. Dawn is conceived in the womb of midnight.

"So Moses stayed there with the Lord forty days and forty nights, neither eating nor drinking, and wrote down the words of the covenant, the Ten Words, on the tablets. At length Moses came down from Mount Sinai with the two stone tablets of the

Tokens in his hands, and when he descended, he did not know that the skin of his face shone because he had been speaking with the Lord" (Exodus 34:28, 29, NEB).

This, then, shall be your legacy of the glory of God, Moses. The law you hold in your hand will be a negative glory, showing you what God is by revealing what he does not want you to be. The promise you hold in your heart will be a positive glory as God leads you upward and onward to the promised land. The light that shines upon your face will be God's reflective glory as others see the presence of God shining in your own life.

Perhaps you did not get what you were expecting when you prayed to see God's glory, Moses, but you have received enough for your lifetime and for all the lifetimes of all those who have come after you. Even in this day, we are indebted to you for asking God to let us see and know enough of himself "for the living of these days" and enough to let us know there is infinitely more yet to come.

EPILOGUE:
BUT THEN FACE TO FACE

All the questions have not been answered and all the problems have not been solved, but in that vivid encounter between God and Moses on the windswept slopes of Sinai I have discovered a faith pattern for both my search and my satisfaction.

Openly and unashamedly I acknowledge my desire to know more, my need to belong, and my request to see God's glory. I know these are not my yearnings alone, but "the hidden depths of many a heart."

Carefully and prayerfully I intend to read with understanding the sign of his passing goodness, the sign of his grace community, and the sign of his given name. I am learning that when I am sincerely open to receive the truth, "he will make it plain."

Gratefully and resolutely I will take my stand with God in a place beside him, I will accept the darkness of the crevice in the rock, and I will bless the hand that shelters me with its cover. I am trying to benefit from the unpleasant but necessary experiences "in the cleft of the rock."

Humanly and humbly I must accept the back of God as the only revelation I can expect in this life, looking for his footprints in the paths of history. I must also understand that it is through his mercy and concern for his children that his face is "hid from our eyes."

Wisely and aggressively I should respond to his revelation with involved commitment, living out his negative glory through his commandments and directions, living up to his positive glory in new horizons of aspiration, and living in his reflective glory that ought to be mine as a radiant pilgrim. I know that although I must work in the shadow of God's back, he has given me sufficient grace "for the living of these days."

Yet the vision is still incomplete, the knowledge is still partial, and I still see "through a glass darkly." Even with the increased wisdom and new insights I gained from Moses, I would be left in the night of despair because of this shadowy incompleteness—except for one bright, overpowering fact: the story is not over!

Paul did not put a period at the end of his observation that we see through a glass darkly. This is not the end of the sentence. The full reading shouts with hope and victory: "For now we see through a glass, darkly; *but then face to face*: now I know in part; but then shall I know even as also I am known."

The promise to the Christian is not merely that he

shall philosophically understand the concepts of deity better as he matures in faith in this life. More than that, it is the blessed assurance that beyond this life he shall continue to exist in a conscious relationship with God, a relationship not of faith alone, but of sight. At last he shall see God face to face.

Perhaps the most vivid description of heaven is that it is the place where God finally turns around. The faithful followers who have prayed to his back, walked in his footprints, searched for his signs in the otherness of his creation and in the reflection of his creatures will be rewarded by knowing his full glory and beholding him face to face.

It will be more than a visual encounter; it will mean an answering of questions, a discovering of ultimate truths, a completing of the puzzles. "Now I know in part; but then shall I know even as also I am known." Let no one say that man is not supposed to know the mysteries of life and the full nature of God. He was created to know and love God; was made in his image to reflect his glory. Sin has obscured that knowledge and love and image and glory. Someday sin shall exist no more, and in God's presence we shall at last know all that we were created and fashioned to know.

In this imperfect interim world of sin and veiled knowledge, we know that we are the children of God, but we realize that we have not come into our full inheritance. "Beloved, now are we the sons of God, and it doth not yet appear what we shall be: but we know that, when he shall appear, we shall be like him; for we shall see him as he is" (1 John 3:2).

When we see him as he really is, the most unbe-
lievably glorious thing shall happen: we shall be like
him! That reflective glory which has only occasionally shone from our lives shall burst forth with his
full brightness. What one thing would you most desire to be or have in God's heaven? Without hesitation the Christian should immediately reply, "I want
to be like Jesus," and that is exactly what God has
promised that we shall receive. So to "see him as he
is" does not mean simply that we shall stand and
stare at his perfect beauty throughout all eternity,
but rather that "we shall be like him." His perfection, completeness, and glory shall be ours also.

To be in his likeness should be and will be the ultimate satisfaction for the child of God. Even the ancient psalmist knew this highest of all ambitions. "As
for me, I will behold thy face in righteousness: I shall
be satisfied, when I awake, with thy likeness" (Psalm
17:15).

In the last chapter of the Bible we receive yet another promise of seeing God face to face, and that
promise speaks of permanent relationship, eternal
service, and bright majesty. "And there shall be no
more curse: but the throne of God and of the Lamb
shall be in it; and his servants shall serve him: *And
they shall see his face*; and his name shall be in their
foreheads. And there shall be no night there; and
they need no candle, neither light of the sun; for the
Lord God giveth them light: and they shall reign for
ever and ever" (Revelation 22:3-5).

If I believe the promises of God and sincerely expect to see him in his glory face to face, to know as I

am known, to be like him, and to reign with him forever and ever, I can walk in contentment for a little
while, living in faith with the revelation of the back
of God.

Only faintly now I see Him,
With the darkling veil between,
But a blessed day is coming,
When His glory shall be seen.

Face to face I shall behold Him,
Far beyond the starry sky;
Face to face in all His glory,
I shall see Him by and by!

from the hymn
Face to Face with Christ;
by Mrs. Frank A. Breck